PRAISE FOR

Becoming Ginger Rogers

"This is such a great analogy . . . how performing fearlessly in the ballroom world can impact one's courage and perspective in the business world. Patrice Tanaka's inspiring memoir about the lessons she learned on the dance floor and how she applied them to her life and career is a joy to read."

—NINA DISESA, chairman
and chief creative officer, McCann New York and
author of *Seducing the Boys Club*

"PR executive Patrice Tanaka writes in graceful, lively prose of her transformation from the depressed, repressed perfectionist known at work as the 'Ayatollah Tanaka' to a ballroom dancing champion she thinks of as 'SambaGrl.' Tanaka's toe-tapping tale of how she awakens to the rhythms of her body and learns to dance through her mistakes—at work as well as in the ballroom—shines with inspiration. It may even send you off to buy a sequined dress and some Ginger Rogers shoes of your own."

—ALICE SCHROEDER, best-selling author,
The Snowball: Warren Buffett and the Business of Life

"Becoming Ginger Rogers . . . is about performing full-out and fearlessly in the ballroom world and adopting that approach to great success in the business world. As her client of more than a decade, I can vouch for that being the case. Patrice has written a joyful and inspiring memoir about the lessons learned from competitive ballroom dancing that have helped her to a richly rewarding business and personal life."

—CARRIE SCHWAB-POMERANTZ, president,
Charles Schwab Foundation

"If you're a *Dancing with the Stars* fan, you'll love this book about ballroom dancing and how it transformed Patrice Tanaka's life and made her a happier woman and more successful CEO."

—EDYTA SLIWINSKA, ballroom champion,
Dancing with the Stars, seasons 1-10

"Within the public relations community Patrice Tanaka is acclaimed for her firm's outrageously creative marketing campaigns. Not satisfied that she was living life to the fullest, she started lessons in ballroom dancing. In her compelling *Becoming Ginger Rogers: How Ballroom Dancing Made Me a Happier Woman, Better Partner, and Smarter CEO* she reports how she reached stardom in her newfound hobby while morphing her into a more effective manager and boss. Once I started reading, I couldn't stop!"

—HAROLD BURSON, founder chairman,
Burson-Marsteller

"Patrice and I have lots in common: both of us started public relations agencies, and both of us became competitive ballroom dancers. That's why this frank and insightful autobiography touches me. It's more than a thoughtful account of these endeavors: through her courage and sense of purpose she makes us see what love and determination can achieve."

—MADELINE DE VRIES HOOPER,
founder, DeVries PR

"If you've ever thought about learning to ballroom dance, this inspiring book by Patrice Tanaka will convince you to run not walk to your nearest dance studio."

—JOHN KIMMINS, president,
Arthur Murray Dance Studios

PATRICE
TANAKA

Becoming

Ginger

Rogers

How Ballroom Dancing
Made Me a Happier Woman,
Better Partner, and Smarter CEO

BENBELLA BOOKS, INC • DALLAS, TEXAS

BenBella

BenBella Books, Inc.
10300 N. Central Expressway, Suite 400
Dallas, TX 75231
www.benbellabooks.com
Send feedback to feedback@benbellabooks.com

Printed in the United States of America
10 9 8 7 6 5 4 3 2 1
Library of Congress Cataloging-in-Publication Data is available for this title.
ISBN 978-1-936661-03-9

Editing by Debbie Harmsen
Copyediting by Lisa Miller
Proofreading by Michael Fedison
Cover design by Ted Mauseth / MausethDesign
Text design and composition by Elyse Strongin, Neuwirth & Associates, Inc.
Printed by Bang Printing

Distributed by Perseus Distribution
perseusdistribution.com

To place orders through Perseus Distribution:
Tel: 800-343-4499
Fax: 800-351-5073
E-mail: orderentry@perseusbooks.com

Significant discounts for bulk sales are available. Please contact Glenn Yeffeth at glenn@benbellabooks.com or (214) 750-3628.

Dedication

To my teachers, Emmanuel Pierre-Antoine and Tony Scheppler, for bringing me unimaginable joy through my dancing, and to countless others who supported me on this journey, including my executive coach, Suzanne Levy; my amazing colleagues at CRT/tanaka and PT&Co.; my friends in the "real" world and the ballroom world; my wonderful coauthor, Lynette Padwa; my indefatigable agent, Fredrica Friedman; the highly creative and collaborative team at BenBella Books, in particular, my editor, Debbie Harmsen; my late husband, "Mr. Sweetheart" Assadulloh Hakiek; and my loving parents, June and Ichiro Tanaka, who made all things possible.

Contents

Becoming

Ginger

Rogers

CHAPTER 1

The Whirl of Manhattan

"Life may not be the party we hoped for, but while we're here we should dance."

—Anonymous

$\mathcal{T}$he gleaming Dyson DC07 stood on a chair at the head of our conference table, the better to inspire us. This was no ordinary vacuum cleaner. The Dyson upright vacuum looked like a bulbous yellow rocket mounted in a shiny gray launch pad. Where a standard vacuum would have had a compartment for a bag, the Dyson had a clear plastic canister. Within that canister was a spinning funnel of yellow "cyclones" that whirled the dirt up into the head of the rocket. It put on quite a show—for an appliance.

The Dyson was already a hit in Europe but was unknown in the States, and our public relations firm, PT&Co., had been hired to introduce it to America. Winning the campaign was a huge boost to both our morale and our balance sheet in the limp year following 9/11. The six partners seated around the table were survivors—not of the attack, which had taken place just two miles from our office, but of the fallout that had sapped businesses in Manhattan ever since. The Dyson could dramatically change things for us.

Sir James Dyson, CEO and inventor of the Dyson DC07, was hiring an ad agency as well as our public relations firm. I always took it as a personal challenge to make our PR efforts at least as powerful as the ad campaign—ideally, more so. The mission of public relations is to attract attention to an organization, an individual, or a product by creating newsworthy stories, causes, or events. A great PR campaign can create tremendous free publicity without the use of paid advertisements. Whenever I pitched prospective clients I liked to tell them, "PR is the Hamburger Helper of the marketing mix. We can help stretch your marketing dollars at a fraction of the cost of advertising." With the Dyson campaign, we would have our work cut out for us. It was an impressive piece of household technology, to be sure, but it was still a vacuum cleaner. Even the humble microwave reminded people of food. A vacuum cleaner reminded them of dirt. And housework.

Ellen LaNicca, the head of our Home and Housewares practice, was in charge of the account, and we were gathered in the conference room to hear her plan for promoting the Dyson. She stood next to the vacuum, took a deep breath, and began.

"There is no Mr. Hoover," Ellen intoned. "There is no Mr. Eureka. There's a Mr. Oreck, but he's a grandpa. And then there is Sir James Dyson, a British inventor so cool that he looks like an actor playing an inventor. The James Bond of bagless technology. Creator of a vacuum cleaner that's as cool as he is, almost a piece of sculpture." She leaned forward, locking eyes with each of us as she delivered her pitch. We grinned back at her, enjoying the show. "This vacuum will forever change our expectations of what such a tool should look like and how it should perform," she continued. "It actually expels *clean air*."

"How do we introduce this extraordinary appliance?" she challenged us. "Who is our target audience?"

She answered her own question: "The fashion world. Design influencers. Early adopters and techno geeks." She paused.

"And where is the best place to do that?"

"Where?" prompted Frank de Falco.

"Fashion Week! Here in New York."

"Brilliant!" I agreed. "How?"

"That's why we're here today," said Ellen. "Let's figure out how to get high fashion and vacuum cleaners together. There's got to be a way."

The Dyson DC07 was aggressively stylish, almost intimidating. Perfect for fashionistas and design lovers. But the vacuums couldn't propel themselves down a runway—they'd have to be pushed by models. That would definitely be a fashion first. The idea was edgy, funny, and would make a terrific photo. Most important, launching the Dyson at Fashion Week, which was coming up in September, would instantly create excitement for the low-interest category of vacuum cleaners. If we pulled off a successful launch, we could end 2002 on a high note.

The spectacle that is New York Fashion Week takes place twice a year. Until 2010, when it moved to the Lincoln Center, it was held in a series of white tents set up in Bryant Park, off Fifth Avenue. This is where the world's top designers debut their spring and fall collections, and each show is strictly invitation-only. We wanted to place the Dyson with a designer who was young, innovative, and always attracting plenty of media attention. After much research, we settled on one of the renegades of the fashion world—actress/

designer Tara Subkoff, and her label, Imitation of Christ. Subkoff was famous for her provocative runway shows—during her tenure at the label she staged events at an East Village funeral parlor and at Sotheby's auction house, among other odd locales. One season she had the models sit in the audience and made fashion editors walk the runway.

In September 2002 Subkoff was again shunning the white tents in favor of a more unique venue—an empty retail space she transformed into a series of vignettes. Each vignette showcased one of the pieces of clothing she was debuting, and each was a commentary on women at home. We couldn't have asked for a more perfect setting for our vacuum cleaner.

On the day of the event, Ellen went to the venue a couple of hours before showtime to check on our vignette. She'd been gone only twenty minutes when my phone rang, flashing her cell number.

"Hi, Ellen. Everything okay? Are the Dysons there?"

"Oh, they're here," she replied. "And the models are here. Three gorgeous, six-foot Russian amazons."

"Great!"

"You know what's not here? Their shirts. The models are topless."

"What?"

"Imitation of Christ wants the models to be vacuuming in a fake living room, wearing nothing but stilettos and tiny cashmere hot pants."

The image was so bizarre that it took me a minute to absorb it.

"Does it look tawdry?"

"Not really tawdry, but maybe, um, provocative."

"Are they doing anything vulgar with the vacuums?"

Ellen laughed a little nervously. "No, of course not. Actually, I better start training them now. We don't have much time."

I got in a cab and raced to the site. The place was already packed with media, people from the nightclub scene, designers, and thirty or forty photographers. It was shoulder to shoulder, everyone pressing forward to see what Imitation of Christ was offering this year. I made my way to the staging area behind the vignettes and spied little five-foot-two Ellen attempting to teach the six-foot Russian models key message points about the Dyson DC07. They spoke no English.

"Watch me!" she finally pleaded. "This is how you turn it on. You have to step on it here." Ellen's head was exactly breast-high to the models, and as one of them bent to turn on the Dyson, her boobs slapped Ellen in the face. Poor Ellen turned deep red and blinked a few times, then continued her instructions: "Don't roll the vacuum over the cord. Say, 'Look at the cyclones.'"

"Look at the cyclones," the models gamely repeated, taking a few practice runs with the vacuums. Their long, glistening limbs and perfect round breasts were compelling, but so was the whirling cyclonic action of the Dysons. It was too late to call London and get this development okayed by Dyson's people. The show would have to go on. I backed out of the staging area and squeezed to the side of the vignette space, awaiting the models' entrance.

A few minutes later our nearly naked Russian beauties strutted out, pushing their Dyson vacuums. Cries of pleasure burst from the crowd, especially from the men, who were delighted to see breasts *and* an amazing new gadget. All around me I heard comments like, "I wish my girlfriend vacuumed that way!" "Do you need to be dressed like that to make the vacuum work?" and, "That's hot—both the hot pants and the vacuum."

Lots of people wanted to know, "What *is* that?" They were fascinated by the swirling dust inside the clear canister. When someone asked to try it out, Ellen went backstage, got a few more Dysons, and let people take turns vacuuming. She stayed there until the wee hours of the morning, then called London to prepare the Dyson team for whatever fallout might occur. "I told them it's not going to be vulgar but it is sexual," Ellen reported. "They're okay with it. For now."

By the next morning a photo of topless models pushing Dyson vacuums was the shot sent round the world. The *New York Times* ran a piece depicting the scene in a simple line drawing. *Women's Wear Daily* put the photo on the cover. As we had hoped, the fashion and design "influentials" who had attended the show started to talk about the Dyson, igniting a buzz. We got such great coverage from the event that we were able to get the vacuums included in the celebrity presenter gift baskets for the Emmy Awards, which took place during the same time frame as the launch. Those lavish gift baskets always attract a lot of media coverage. When the basket was featured on the *Today* show and Al Roker spotted the bright yellow-and-gray Dyson vacuum, he said, "Wow! I want one of those." We immediately sent him one, and he followed up with a handwritten note saying, "Thank you so much for my Dyson. I'm glad I now have a product that really does suck." This was a reference to the cyclonic technology of Dyson vacuums, which meant they would never lose suction over time—the reason that other vacuums become less effective the longer you use them.

Our campaign included much more than the initial launch. In fewer than eight months, we generated more than 525 print and broadcast stories on the Dyson DC07. The vacuum exceeded its U.S. sales forecast by 160 percent, and *Time* magazine named it 2002's "Best Invention." The Dyson catapulted from no market share to category leader in fewer than eighteen months. Sir James was pleased, and so were we.

♪

At the time we introduced the Dyson to America, I had been in public relations for twenty-five years. I started out in Hawaii but had moved to New York in my twenties. Although I grew up in Honolulu, the daughter of second-generation Japanese Americans, I never felt at home in the tropics. While the other girls were giggling about cute local boys who spoke pidgin English, I was dreaming of life in Manhattan. That was where I belonged. I knew it from the age of nine.

As a grade schooler I lived in the make-believe world of black-and-white films of the 1930s and '40s, which played regularly on television. In that world, elegant men and women, dressed to the nines, danced until dawn at glittering nightclubs, and talked on white telephones in their art deco penthouse apartments. I longed to be one of those tall, slim, beautiful women.

—

Ginger was light and luminous—she floated in Fred's arms, and when he gently dipped her, the gown fanned out like lush, elegant plumage. I was awestruck by their poetry in motion.

—

It was the dancing in those movies that enthralled me more than anything. I adored scenes like the one in *Top Hat* where Fred Astaire and Ginger Rogers danced to the song "Cheek to Cheek," he in tails and she in a white, feathered gown. Fred and Ginger flowed together effortlessly, their movements a perfectly synchronized expression of their longing for each other. Ginger was light and luminous—she floated in Fred's arms, and when he gently dipped her, the gown fanned out like lush, elegant plumage. I was awestruck by their poetry in motion.

In another of my favorite films, Flying Down to Rio, a flamboyant nightclub waiter tells Fred and Ginger that in Brazil, "the American foxtrot is considered too tame, too dull. Our people prefer the carioca!"

"You mean they prefer it in public?" asks a slightly scandalized Ginger.

"Si, señorita! Everybody in Rio!" The couple proceeds to tear up the dance floor with an improvised "carioca" performed with foreheads touching and feet flying. A mash-up of samba, foxtrot, rumba, and tap, the scene sparked in me a lifelong love of the samba. The setting of fabled Rio de Janeiro, with aerial shots of Sugarloaf Mountain and Corcovado Mountain, topped by the famous statue *Christ the Redeemer*, stoked my yearning for travel. I could hardly wait until I was old enough to flee Hawaii for the bright lights of New York and beyond.

To satisfy my wanderlust, I worked while in high school so that I could pay for summer vacations to Japan and Western Samoa. In college I spent three months hitchhiking across Europe, and after earning a degree in English and journalism, I took a job writing for a tourism newspaper in Hawaii.

While I was writing for the paper, the Inter-Continental Hotel in Maui offered me a position as its public relations director. As soon as I grasped what it meant, I knew it was the right fit for me. In public relations you didn't just report on the news, you dreamed up ways to generate stories about your clients. You created new and improved realities for them—such as positioning them as market leaders, visionaries, innovators, or leaders in social responsibility.

Compared to now, the pace of PR was leisurely. I used snail mail to distribute press releases and photos to the media, and

I banged out copy on an IBM Correcting Selectric II, at that time a state-of-the-art typewriter because it used a correction ribbon to erase typos—far superior to painting over your mistakes with white-out! Before the digital age, assembling a press kit involved lots of time-consuming, hands-on work. I shot my own photos of the visiting celebrity guests who stayed at our world-class resort, and then I sent the film out to be developed, selected photos from contact sheets, had stills printed, and finally mailed them with identifying captions to the media. If the deadline was tight, I'd send a messenger.

Twenty-five years later, in 2002, I was living in Manhattan and had my own PR agency. We were just getting started on a wild digital ride that was breathtaking, unstoppable, and had no end in sight. Computers had accelerated the speed and flexibility with which we could produce multimedia news releases embedded with website links, digital images, graphics, video and audio clips, any type of collateral we might need, and all the other tools of a public relations campaign.

But it was the Internet that totally revolutionized the industry. Stories that were once local now had the potential to instantly become global. Anyone with an Internet connection could easily search for obscure news and information on every topic. It soon became clear that this would be both a boon and a curse to people and organizations in need of public relations—a curse because the misstatements and misdeeds of anyone, from the CEO to a line employee, could be captured and communicated for all the world to see. For PR agencies, both the good and the bad press meant more work.

We had made our name at PT&Co. and earned more than 180 industry awards, by creating innovative brand PR and cause-related marketing campaigns designed to burnish our clients' reputation while making a difference on health and social issues such as domestic violence, breast cancer, literacy, and hunger relief. Our credo was, "Great work, great workplace, great communities that work." The Internet promised us limitless ways to pursue those goals.

In 2002 the possibilities of the Internet and social networking were just beginning to emerge. MySpace and Second Life made their debut in 2003, followed by Facebook and Flickr in 2004. YouTube wouldn't be launched until 2005, and Twitter in 2006, but we could email images, text, and links to videos the moment we produced them. Our goal with the Dyson account had been to get that stunning vacuum cleaner in front of millions of eyeballs alongside Fashion Week's hottest couture designs. We succeeded in large part because of the Internet's instant global reach.

The Dyson's triumphant rollout at Fashion Week lifted our spirits, especially since it provided a distraction from the relentless one-year anniversary stories about 9/11. Across the country things seemed pretty much back to normal. Not in New York. The Twin Towers had been visible from some of our office windows, and the empty sky where they once stood was a daily reminder of the catastrophe and its aftermath. I know I wasn't the only person who trained myself to avoid those windows.

When the attacks happened, millions of people around the world experienced it together. Everyone remembers switching on the television, seeing the smoking towers, and not comprehending what they were looking at because it couldn't be real. It was like the first sickening moments after a car crash. In New York that dreadful feeling ballooned, swallowed everything, and didn't go away. We all knew someone who had died or lost a loved one. Nothing fell back into place.

Mayor Giuliani closed the city for a week after 9/11, during which we all attempted to work from home. When we returned to the office I called everyone into the meditation room, a sunny, carpeted space with a wall of windows and no furniture, just pillows on the floor. I felt I had to say something about the disaster; we couldn't simply go back to work without discussing the matter. The entire staff of nearly fifty people was gathered in the room. Among them were the six PT&Co. partners who had been working together for fifteen years or more.

Ellen LaNicca, the star of the Dyson campaign, was the partner with whom I'd been working the longest. A petite, brown-haired, freckle-faced Irish American from Long Island, Ellen looked about fourteen when we first met, yet she comported herself like a seasoned PR professional. Her poise and perfect diction were a bit daunting, but I knew a winner when I met one and I wanted her on my team. She was upbeat—sometimes a little too upbeat—driven, bright, and extremely creative.

Frank de Falco, our resident intellectual and culturally literate New Yorker, was a handsome, slightly round-faced Italian American with a beard and a full head of thick black hair. A gifted writer, he was also so shamelessly sloppy that he referred to himself as "the Ted Bundy of serial typos." It drove perfectionist me up a wall. Frank responded to my frustration by dubbing me "Ayatollah Tanaka."

Maria Kalligeros was a tall, beautiful, and brilliant woman of Greek descent. She and I had similar work habits: obsessive, competitive, and precise. But when it came to our worldviews, we couldn't have been more different. I was one of those "glass half full" types; Maria was the opposite. Yet she and I probably laughed together more than any two people at the agency.

If Maria and I had opposite temperaments, Evelyn Calleja was my emotional twin. Our CFO was a short, heavy, beautiful, and vivacious Latina who, before working in accounting had tried her hand at numerous vocations, including stand-up comedienne, bar owner, and professional dog groomer. A healer and psychic, she would lead us in group meditation sessions when she wasn't too absorbed in handling agency finances.

Every company needs an organizational whiz, and ours was John Frazier. A tall, lanky southerner from Baton Rouge, he could wrangle any project. He even oversaw the design and build-out of our sunlit, loft-like office in the West Village near the Meatpacking District. John was somewhat shy and introverted for a PR professional. Like me, he was a die-hard liberal and a compassionate soul. I loved him dearly, but he could drive me crazy with his obstinacy if he didn't want to do something.

The sixth founding partner of PT&Co. was Fran Kelly, a native of Queens. Fran's strength was client management—she was both highly capable and fearless, and she bore the considerable stresses of her job lightly. Fran was devoted to her husband and two daughters—her pride and joy. She knew she had to save some energy for them, so more than the rest of us she seemed able to rein in the work-related angst.

Sitting together in the meditation room that first day back after 9/11, longtime partners and young staffers alike shared a similar shell-shocked expression. The sky out-side our windows was still dirty with ash, and the smell of burned plastic and metal still clogged our throats. I wasn't sure what I could say that would make any difference to them, but as the leader I had to try. I kept thinking about those nearly three thousand people who reported for work that morning at the Twin Towers, not knowing that this day would be their last. I thought about the future plans they all had, unaware that they had no future beyond 9:59 a.m., when the South Tower collapsed, and 10:28 a.m., when the North Tower fell.

"I'm sure what happened last week has made all of us aware how important it is to live each day fully," I began. "Life is sometimes cut short by events we have no control over, and maybe it's impossible to ever really be prepared for that. But I know that the last thing I want for myself, or any of us, is for our last moments on earth to be filled with anger or resentment toward one another. I'm asking that we all recommit to creating a more joy-filled workplace com-munity at PT&Co. by treating one another in a kinder and more gentle way."

⌣

*"Life is sometimes cut short by events
we have no control over, and maybe it's
impossible to ever really be prepared
for that. But I know that the last thing
I want for myself, or any of us, is for
our last moments on earth to be filled
with anger or resentment toward one
another."*

⌣

Evelyn suggested that we all commit to eliminating toxicity in our workplace by not judging one another, not rushing to lay blame when something went wrong, and not arguing over petty issues. She asked that we all leave our egos outside the door as a way to create room for greater joy. We all nodded in agreement, thinking of those people in the Twin Towers whose final moments were spent with their coworkers. Evelyn then led the group in a brief meditation, first focusing us on our breathing and then guiding us in relaxing every part of our body to help ease us into our first day back at the office.

The rest of 2001 was spent trying to deal with the shock of how much our world had changed overnight by this act of terrorism, and trying to come to grips with a new sense of vulnerability we felt as New Yorkers and Americans. To make matters worse, business essentially fell off a cliff in October, and we had no idea when or if it would bounce back. We began 2002 by reducing shareholder salaries by 20 percent and employee salaries by 10 percent to avoid layoffs. We froze all raises for the foreseeable future. It wasn't an auspicious start to the new year, which we all knew would be about more work and less pay. We'd have to keep pitching prospective clients and dreaming up ways to attract new business, which was just as hard and a lot less rewarding than actually working on a campaign. In the first six months of 2002, we lost more than a third of our billings, and all travel accounts evaporated.

The days were long—it wasn't unusual for me to clock sixty-hour weeks. I had worked those hours for many years as I built the agency, but back then I was inspired by the challenge. Now it was just a burden. In addition to the anxiety of not knowing when business would rebound, I couldn't shake my melancholy. No one talked about it much—New Yorkers are supposed to be cynical, cocky survivors, not whiners—but we were all feeling it. On the taxi ride home each day, as the distractions of the job faded, my mind would roll back to the attacks. I'd look out the window at the pedestrians hurrying down the streets and wonder about them. Whom had they lost? Did they feel as sad as I did? Sometimes the scene reminded me of old black-and-white films—not the glamorous musicals with Fred and Ginger, but grim noirish tales I had never much liked and certainly did not want to be living. And unlike a movie, I had no idea when this would end.

—

I couldn't shake my melancholy. No one talked about it much—New Yorkers are supposed to be cynical, cocky survivors, not whiners—but we were all feeling it.

—

Amid all this uncertainty, the success of the Dyson campaign in 2002 lifted everyone's spirits at the office, including mine. But work was only one part of my life, and even there, the lift was only a temporary boost in a season of very low lows. Also, success at work presented a sad irony: I could make a vacuum cleaner rule the runway at Fashion Week, but my own life sucked (and not in the sexy vacuum way). I was exhausted, depressed, and certainly not sleek and shiny like the fabulous Dyson. That vacuum was sexier than me.

CHAPTER 2

The Arabian Prince

"Dancing is a vertical expression of a horizontal passion."
—George Bernard Shaw

$\mathcal{M}$y home had always provided a refuge from the stress of daily life. The apartment where I lived was on the twenty-sixth floor of a high-rise overlooking the Hudson River. It featured exactly the sparkling penthouse view I had envisioned when I was a girl in Honolulu, but instead of art deco furniture, I had decorated it like a tropical retreat. The odd thing was, as soon as I escaped Hawaii, I started to re-create it in Manhattan. I didn't regret leaving, but it was only after I had settled in New York that I understood how deeply rooted I was in the Island sensibility. Towering umbrella plants and palms softened the corners of my living room, and potted orchids graced the tables and windowsills. Throughout the apartment there were collections of seashells, painted tropical fish, beach glass, books, Japanese pottery, framed photos, and large paintings of placid-faced Hawaiian women in languid poses. The furniture was 1930s Island style—deep, low, streamlined rattan with thick, white duck cloth cushions. The windows overlooking the Hudson suffused the room with pearly light in the winter and framed magnificent sunsets year-round.

The first sight that met my eyes when I walked through the door each evening was a painting I had always treasured—a portrait of me at age twenty-two, wearing a tangerine tank top and a choker with a big white flower. My hair cascaded over my shoulders, wild and thick, and a few loose strands fell across my face. Many years had passed since the portrait had been painted, and naturally I had aged, but no one would mistake me for that girl's mother. I looked more like her jolly maiden aunt. Gone was the long hair and tropical attire. Now I wore the typical New York female executive's uniform of black pantsuit with a neutral blouse. I had gained thirty pounds, cut my hair in a short wash-and-wear style, and wore black-framed glasses. The young woman in the painting was sultry. She looked directly at the artist; she knew how to flirt. Sultry, young Patrice Tanaka had liked sex and indulged in lots of it. Maiden Aunt Patrice hadn't had sex in eight years.

Past the foyer, I usually spied the creator of that portrait resting in one of the living room chairs, watching television. His face would brighten when he saw me, and no matter how weary I was, I always smiled back. My husband of sixteen years (and love of my life for twenty-one) was consistently cheerful and still looked vigorous. He had the easy grace of someone who had always been handsome, and he often told me that despite some bad breaks, he felt as if he had been born lucky.

I first caught sight of Assad in the fall of 1982 at a Greek restaurant where he was working as a waiter. For me, the moment unfolded like a scene in a movie—the lights dimmed, the soundtrack rose to a sweeping crescendo, and the room receded except for the spot where this one man stood in a shaft of light. He looked as if he had stepped right out of *1001 Arabian Nights* or *The Thief of Baghdad*—tall and muscular and drop-dead gorgeous. I always knew that my beloved would be an exotic Arabian prince like the heroes in those swashbuckling adventure films. After spending a couple of weeks getting to know Assad, I saw how beautiful he was on the inside, too. Listening to the stories he told about his background, I could tell he was a man of character who had been tested in ways most of my friends could barely imagine.

Assad was from Afghanistan, the son of a highly respected judge. He had been a student at Kabul Polytechnic when he and seventeen of his classmates were forcibly taken from their dormitory one evening by Russian soldiers when the Soviet Union invaded Afghanistan in December 1979. Assad and his friends were given the terrible choice of either conscription into the Russian army, or imprisonment. They chose the army, but eventually deserted and joined local Afghan villagers who were fighting against their former Russian battalion. Finally the students fled across the border into Pakistan and later to India. Once there, Assad successfully petitioned the U.S. government to accept him as a political refugee. He had studied English while growing up, dreaming that one day he might come to America. I doubt he thought he would arrive here alone and poor. Assad was working at the Greek restaurant while attending Brooklyn Polytechnic to earn the degree in civil engineering that had been interrupted by the Soviet invasion of Afghanistan.

Assad's tales about his homeland were not always grim. He also captivated me with family legends that sounded like ancient parables. One of my favorites starred Assad's grandfather, Hyakul. Good looks ran in the family, and Hyakul was no exception. Sometime in the early 1900s, Hyakul and a group of Afghani men had taken part in an uprising against an unpopular ruler. The group stormed and looted the palace in Kabul, where the ruler lived. Most of the men took jewelry, artwork, and other valuables from the palace. Assad's grandfather, however, was mesmerized by his reflection in a tall mirror mounted on a carved wooden stand. This was the only treasure Hyakul stole from the palace, carrying it on his head and walking many miles back to his village. Neighbors came to admire the mirror, which was set in a prominent place in Hyakul's home. One day a distant relative—an ignorant, unworldly man—came to visit. Upon seeing his own reflection in the mirror, he went to embrace the stranger who was approaching him, arms similarly outstretched. In that rough embrace, the treasured mirror broke. So, too, did the heart of Assad's grandfather.

The combination of Assad's good looks, exotic background, and generous heart was impossible to resist. Within a few months we were inseparable. A fairy-tale quality infused the romance, for good and ill. Our relationship was very passionate, and stayed that way for a long time, partly fueled by the negative side of the fairy tale: ours was a "forbidden" affair because Assad hadn't told his parents about us. He felt guilty about falling in love with a Christian, Japanese American, New York entrepreneur (a rarer, more type A breed than the typical businesswoman). I was a far cry from the subservient Muslim wife his mother was hoping to select for him. His parents were still in Afghanistan, so he simply didn't mention me. He'd talk to his mother on the phone, never confessing that he was in a relationship, yet consistently refusing to meet the potential wives his mother had chosen. Assad's mother fully expected that she would select a wife for him and that he would return to Afghanistan to meet and marry her, and then leave her there to care for his parents. After those biweekly conversations, Assad would be wracked by guilt about us because he couldn't acquiesce to his mother's greatest wish to find him a bride. So he would respond by breaking up with me. A few days later we'd be back together. It was wrenching.

———

A fairy-tale quality infused the romance, for good and ill. Our relationship was very passionate, and stayed that way for a long time, partly fueled by the negative side of the fairy tale: ours was a "forbidden" affair because Assad hadn't told his parents about us.

———

As painful as the breakups were, they actually heightened the longing and romance of our situation. In the three-hankie tearjerkers I grew up on, like *Now, Voyager*, and *Casablanca*, the greatest love affairs were always either noble and unrequited, or doomed. Assad, meanwhile, was caught in a different drama. Accustomed to being his mother's favorite child, he knew how devastated she would be to learn that he would not be marrying an Afghani girl from a good family who would bear her many grandchildren and cater to her like a maidservant. Assad often said that his path to heaven was between the two feet of his parents, meaning that salvation could be attained only by obeying their every wish. I clearly recall the two of us huddled under the covers of his bed in Astoria, Queens, feeling scared and not knowing how this story was going to end. Would we ultimately be forced to part? Or would some miracle happen so that we could marry and grow old together here in America?

We finally did marry in 1987 after a stormy five-year courtship. For the first four years of our marriage, his parents still had no idea I existed. Assad worried that if he didn't tell them in person they might never speak to him again. At last, in 1991, he traveled to Mecca to rendezvous with them. It was still unsafe for him to return home to Afghanistan, and the war with Russia and its aftermath had made the journey to Mecca all but impossible for most Afghanis. But Assad had arranged for his mother and father to make this pilgrimage, or hajj, which all devout Muslims are supposed to make at least once in their lives. Maybe Assad was wise to wait to tell his parents about me because they were so overjoyed to go on the hajj, and so happy to see Assad after nine years, that, once the initial shock wore off, they accepted the news of our marriage without further objections.

Me with Assad at our wedding. His radiance never faded.

By that time Assad was dealing with a health condition that made his parents' opinion of me seem less important. A year before we married, he had suffered a seizure. Doctors discovered a cancerous tumor in his brain and performed the first of what would eventually be three surgeries. He had radiation therapy and chemotherapy, and over the next fifteen years, countless alternative treatments around the country and in Europe. Throughout, Assad remained surprisingly upbeat. He didn't look any different, other than gaining a little weight and losing a little hair.

Three years after we discovered Assad's tumor, in January 1989, I was diagnosed with cancer myself. I was thirty-seven years old when I had surgery to remove an ovarian cyst. It was at a very early stage, but because of the aggressive nature of ovarian cancer my oncologist kept a close watch on my condition. In January 1990 I had another cyst removed. This time there were complications, and my surgeon was forced to perform a hysterectomy. It seemed that between Assad and me, our married life was going to be an ongoing medical drama with us having alternating surgeries and hospital stays. And there was, in fact, more. In October 1993, several years after we had founded PT&Co., I went in for a routine mammogram. I was immediately diagnosed with ductal carcinoma in situ, microcalcifications in the milk duct. Stunned and in a fog, I headed back to the office. The radiologist had told me it was stage O breast cancer and therefore most likely curable. Still, another cancer diagnosis was a sickening blow. I researched my condition at length, and by the time I went to see my breast surgeon a few days later I had already decided to have a mastectomy. The doctor was visibly relieved when I told him of my decision and confided that if it were his wife, that's what he would counsel her to do. I had a mastectomy to remove my left breast, and reconstructive surgery during the same operation. Fortunately I didn't have to undergo any postoperative therapy. Assad was a kind and patient caretaker to me after each of my surgeries. My friends and colleagues marveled at how strong and upbeat I was. I guess I felt that I had been pretty lucky. My breast and ovarian cancers had both been stage O, so it could have been much worse. Meanwhile, I was gaining weight, probably from the change in my hormones due to the hysterectomy, exacerbated by my worrying about Assad.

I fully recovered from both of my cancers, at least physically. On the surface, Assad also seemed to fare well for many years. But by 2000 he was experiencing serious cognitive deficits. He had a hard time processing requests like, "Can you go to Food Emporium and buy some milk and then pick up your prescription at CVS?" I never knew how a request like that would play out. Assad might go to Food Emporium and buy the milk and then forget to stop at CVS. Or he might ask me to repeat my request several times, trying to mentally process going to Food Emporium and then stopping at CVS. Or he might go to Food Emporium, forget what I asked him to buy, and come home empty-handed. Instead of saying, "I forgot," he'd get angry and deny I had asked him to shop in the first place. In turn I'd get irritated that he had no memory of our conversation, and I'd make him listen as I reconstructed it in detail. I always hoped he'd say, "Oh, now I remember." He never did.

I can't pinpoint exactly when we stopped having sex, but it was probably sometime in 1996. Assad just lost interest. "It's not me," I'd tell myself. "The doctors said the treatments would affect his libido." Slowly I stopped seeing myself as a woman and a sexual creature. I gained weight. I streamlined my beauty regimen by cutting my hair very short and slicking it back so I didn't have to spend time primping and curling it. I wore dark, chunky glasses that I thought were stylish. I looked asexual, and I felt neutered. I was certainly not wearing hot pants and heels while vacuuming my home topless.

Though he had studied civil engineering, Assad never did practice it. He became a painter instead. At the graduation ceremony for his master's degree, he had whispered to me, "Do you know what I really want to be? I want to be an artist."

My heart sank, knowing that it was a low- to no-income career, but I didn't let on. "If that's what you want to do, then you have to go for it," I encouraged him. All these years later, I was glad he had pursued his art, taking classes all over the city and painting in oil, pastel, and acrylic. His paintings covered the walls of our home, and no matter how bad his memory became, he was still able to paint.

Over the years, I spent more and more time tending to Assad's needs, both at home and at work. The care was never-ending, whether it was changing a dressing, dealing with doctors, or battling insurance companies.

One evening during the waning days of September 2002, I walked over to where Assad dozed in front of the television and touched him lightly on the arm. "Hey, Mr. Sweetheart. You should probably get to bed now." Those were our pet names for each other—Mr. and Mrs. Sweetheart. Like so much else, the names were tinged with sadness for me now. This good man, who truly was my Mr. Sweetheart, was becoming sweeter and gentler with each passing day, and less and less like the adventurous, strapping guy I had met twenty years ago.

Whatever dramatic arc I had conjured for our story in the early tumultuous years, I had never foreseen this one. My wifely role had been completely transformed from romantic soul mate and sexy lover to caretaker, cook, nag, and breadwinner. I didn't see any way out of my predicament. I wasn't going to abandon my husband, whom I loved deeply and who could not take care of himself. I felt trapped. Was this how I was going to live the rest of my life, never again feeling like a desirable woman? "Surely this can't be it for me, God," I used to pray. I saw, in time, that God did indeed have more for me.

CHAPTER 3

"What Brings You Joy?"

"While I dance I cannot judge, I cannot hate, I cannot separate myself from life. I can only be joyful and whole. That is why I dance."

—Hans Bos

$\mathcal{W}$hile we were planning the Dyson event, I had noticed something different about our CFO, Evelyn Calleja. She hadn't lost weight but she seemed lighter. Evelyn was always the most adventurous among us—she had tried stand-up comedy, owned a bar, and learned to give Reiki treatments. I wondered what she was up to now. She seemed cheerful, energetic, clear-thinking, and impressively efficient. It was a stark contrast to the bleak and empty feeling I still couldn't seem to shake five months after 9/11. I was beginning to worry that my malaise might turn into full-blown depression. If Evelyn had access to some sort of magic potion, I was willing to try it.

"There's no magic," said Evelyn. "I've been working with an executive coach named Suzanne Levy." Thrilled at how straightforward her solution was, I booked a session right away.

I had barely settled into the chair at Suzanne's office when she got right to the point. "So tell me," she said, "what is your purpose in life?"

I was taken aback, even though I asked prospective employees the same question in every job interview. For years I had a snappy, business-focused response if anyone tossed such a question my way: "Five years, five million dollars in fee income, fifty employees." It was an easy-to-remember mantra, which actually helped us achieve that goal (but in seven years, not five). Nowadays I was in too much of a funk to get excited about a business goal or any other long-term plan. Instead, I started thinking once again about my husband's declining health and the nearly three thousand people who had perished in the Twin Towers attack.

"I'm not talking about your career," Suzanne continued. "I mean your grand mission in life, your true purpose on this planet. Take as long as you want to think about it."

~

I reflected on how I could live my life so that I would be ready to go whenever it was my time. I knew that doing this meant I had to live every moment in a way that was fulfilling in and of itself, not dependent upon some future I might not have.

~

Over the next two weeks, I struggled to come up with a mission that rang true for me and that I could get excited about. I wondered how many people in the World Trade Center had been full of unfulfilled dreams and happiness tied to some future event planned for that weekend, the next summer, or even some years later. I reflected on how I could live my life so that I would be ready to go whenever it was my time. I knew that doing this meant I had to live every moment in a way that was fulfilling in and of itself, not dependent upon some future I might not have.

At my next coaching session, I was ready to share my "grand mission" with Suzanne: "My purpose in life is to choose joy each day, to be mindful of that joy, and to share that joy with others."

No sooner did I end that sentence than Suzanne asked, "So what brings you joy?"

"Dancing." The word popped out of my mouth before I could think, and I must have looked surprised because we both laughed.

"When was the last time you went dancing?" Hard as I tried, I couldn't remember.

"Interesting," said Suzanne. "Your homework assignment is to book yourself a dance lesson before our next session. Do you know the name of a studio?"

"Your homework assignment is to book yourself a dance lesson before our next session."

"Of course," I was able to reply. I did have the name of a dance studio. My friend David Moyer had given it to me two years prior and I had been carrying it around in my Palm Pilot ever since. David was the man responsible for my moving from Maui to New York in 1979. I had been calling PR executive search firms in Manhattan, trying to line up a position before I made the move. David worked at one of these firms, and of all the people I spoke with, he was the nicest. He was also the most honest, telling me, "No one will take you seriously unless you live here. If you really want to do this, quit your job in Hawaii, move to New York, and then start your job search." And that's what I did.

David and I have been friends ever since. He is six foot four and a dead ringer for David Letterman. (He used to work in the same building as Letterman and reported that one time the two of them had been alone in the elevator. "Hey, you look just like me," said Letterman. Always quick on his feet, David retorted, "No, you look just like me.") David's tastes are eclectic, ranging from harpsichord recitals to opera to Scottish dancing. Many of his passions strike me as endearingly quirky, but when he told me that he belonged to a waltz society, I was intrigued. I had written down the name of the studio where he took lessons—Pierre Dulaine.

My homework assignment was looming, but I waited until the last minute to arrange for my dance lesson. It's the perfectionist's way: if you can't do it perfectly, avoid doing it. I had never taken dance lessons as a child, despite the fact that

I practically lived in a pink tutu when I was six. I had not a smidgen of technique to fall back on, so I was pretty sure that my first lesson would be humiliating at best. Two days before my next coaching session, I finally called the Pierre Dulaine Dance Studio. They were able to squeeze me in the following afternoon.

I had been carrying the studio's address around with me all this time because, for me, there was only one type of dance worth learning: ballroom dance. Today millions of people know what ballroom dancing really is thanks to *Dancing with the Stars*—copied in some fashion in more than thirty countries—and the major dances are recognized by young and old alike. However, when I began taking lessons in 2002, the American version of *Dancing with the Stars* was three years away from its debut, and ballroom dancing was unknown to much of the general public. For Generation Xers and baby Boomers like me, it was dancing that our parents or grandparents had done in another era. If people pictured anything when they heard the term "ballroom dance," it was the very formal International Standard style of dancing, where partners held each other closely while sweeping around the dance floor with great precision and speed, the woman arched backward at an alarming angle with a wide, frozen smile on her face.

But ballroom dancing is so much more than that. To me, it symbolizes the Manhattan I had fallen in love with when watching all those old movies, where Fred and Ginger dazzled the crowds at the Stork Club and El Morocco. Of course, by the time I arrived in Manhattan in 1979, those clubs were long gone. CBGB on Bowery Street was the hot scene, and its blaring punk rock was a universe away from the elegant nightlife that had fueled my childhood fantasies. It was a shock to realize that I had lived in New York for more than twenty years and never taken a dance lesson, even though it was the vision of Fred and Ginger that had propelled me here in the first place.

It was a shock to realize that I had lived in New York for more than twenty years and never taken a dance lesson, even though it was the vision of Fred and Ginger that had propelled me here in the first place.

I took a cab to the Pierre Dulaine Dance Studio right after work. I was expecting a spacious ballroom with a grand entrance at street level, but the studio was located on the fourth floor of an undistinguished office building on West Thirty-First Street. Exiting the elevator, I entered a dark, narrow hallway lined with photos of dance world luminaries such as Tommy Tune and Cyd Charisse. There were also photos of a young, debonair Pierre Dulaine and his dance partner, Yvonne Marceau. The couple had been four-time winners of the British Exhibition Championships in the late 1970s and early '80s. In the black-and-white photos, Dulaine looked a bit like Antonio Banderas who, in fact, played the role of Pierre Dulaine in the 2006 film *Take the Lead*. That film was a fictional version of the award-winning documentary *Mad Hot Ballroom*. Both films were inspired by the New York City public school system's "Dancing Classrooms" program, which Pierre had founded in 1994. The program used ballroom dancing to teach fifth-graders about civility and etiquette, and treating one another with dignity and respect. At the time of my first lesson I knew nothing about Pierre's impressive background or "Dancing Classrooms," and *Mad Hot Ballroom* had yet to be filmed.

At the end of the hall sat a reception desk, and just beyond it was a rather shabby sitting area. I informed the friendly young woman at the desk that I was here for a lesson with Mr. Dulaine. Within a few moments, an older version of the beautiful young man in the photos strode out and grasped my hand. His hair was now salt and pepper, but he was still compact and well groomed, and charming in a slightly affected and theatrical way. He led me past the sad, carpeted sitting area, which opened to the dance floor—a long windowless room with mirrored walls. The floor could be divided into two sections by heavy red velvet drapes that hung from the low ceiling. It wasn't exactly the grand ballroom I had envisioned.

Four other couples were on the dance floor, each doing a different dance. Three of the women were about my age, and were dancing with much younger men, whom I assumed were ballroom teachers. One elderly gentleman was dancing with a much younger female dance teacher. The students were all intently focused on trying to follow their teachers' instructions. From the sitting area, people sat chatting and watching the dancers. *Wonderful . . .* an audience. Self-consciousness flooded my body and I stood frozen on the dance floor.

"Did you bring dance shoes?" asked Pierre.

"I brought these," I replied, holding up a pair of low-heeled pumps I had packed for the occasion.

"They'll do for now. Go ahead, put them on."

I quickly slipped into the pumps and Pierre led me to an empty spot at the edge of the floor. He stood about a foot from me and positioned my arms, the right one straight out so he could grasp my hand, the left bent at the elbow with my hand lightly resting on his shoulder.

"We'll begin with the foxtrot," said Pierre. "It is a basic box step. To the right, forward, to the left, and back. Slow-quick-quick. Slow-quick-quick."

I stiffly attempted to follow his lead, feeling like a mario-nette. The simple pattern was trickier than it looked. I tried to concentrate, but I kept peering past Pierre's shoulder to see what the other couples were doing. One teacher and student were moving rhythmically toward each other and back again, swiveling their hips to a bouncy Latin beat.

"That looks fun!" I said. "Can we do that dance?"

"You'll need to learn the basic steps of rhythm dances like the cha cha and rumba before you learn the more challenging steps of samba," replied Pierre. "The foxtrot is one of the most popular smooth dances." I hadn't a clue what *rhythm* or *smooth* meant.

"Slow-quick-quick. Slow-quick-quick," Pierre repeated patiently as he danced me through the foxtrot basic step. My feet seemed disconnected from my brain. For the first thirty minutes I was acutely aware of the other dancers and the people watching me. Had there ever been a slower student? The other women wore short swingy skirts or long, full ones, and my black pantsuit made me feel even more out of place.

By the end of the hour I had finally mastered the box step. I could match it to the music, and for a few brief moments it felt like real dancing. I was winded, my legs hurt, my feet throbbed, and my arms ached. But I signed up for another lesson. On the elevator ride down I mused that for one full hour, I had not thought of a single thing other than the foxtrot.

At my next lesson, Pierre led me through the rumba basics, which, like the foxtrot, followed a simple box step. Instead of "slow-quick-quick," the rhythm was "quick-quick-slow." I had forgotten half of what I had learned the previous week, so it was a good thing the rumba box step wasn't more complex.

Suzanne, my executive coach, was thrilled that she had gotten me onto the dance floor. After that successful first step, she prodded me to do other things for myself that I had neglected while trying to take care of everyone else. Some of these, such as finally setting up my personal banking online, were simple, yet they freed up precious time. A major gift from Suzanne was her encouraging me to say "No" to people if I needed to—especially, "No, I can't do that because I have a dance lesson." Suzanne knew that dance could be the vehicle that transported me to a more joyful existence.

When I arrived at the studio for my third dance lesson, Pierre told me he was partnering me with a new teacher. I wondered if he was shunting me off to someone less experienced, but all uncharitable thoughts vanished when I laid eyes on the matinee idol who was crossing the dance floor in my direction. If I had asked central casting for a teacher, six-foot-four Tony Scheppler would have been that man. Impeccably groomed, from his wavy, jet-black hair to the cut of his pleated trousers and polished shoes, Tony had the look and fashion sensibility of a 1930s heartthrob. I later learned that he had appeared in the wedding reception dance scene of the movie *Mona Lisa Smile* and had proven to be a bit of a challenge to the director because he was better looking than the leading man.

At first, concentrating on my dance steps was even harder because tall, dark, and handsome Tony was quite a distraction. However, it was soon apparent that not only was he a marvelous dancer but also a truly gifted teacher. His passion for dance was infectious, and he had a friendly, easygoing style of instruction. Tony's exaggerated impressions of my mistakes were so funny that I couldn't help but loosen up in my dancing. At the same time, his pantomimes made my missteps perfectly clear, which made it easier for me to improve. After my first lesson with Tony, I stood on the side-walk in front of the studio, chuckling at the foxtrot we had managed to perform all the way through. *I'm not half bad,* I thought to myself. I don't know if it had dawned on me, but I was not only dancing like I'd dreamed of doing as a child, I was laughing again.

⁓

I'm not half bad, I thought to myself.
I don't know if it had dawned on me,
but I was not only dancing like I'd
dreamed of doing as a child, I was
laughing again.

⁓

I learned more about my new teacher in the following weeks. Tony was a former high school football star from Canton, Ohio, who had taken dance lessons as a teenager to learn how to leap higher on the field. He fell in love with dancing, quit football, and quickly became a national ama-teur ballroom dance champion, later turning professional. When I met him, Tony had been dancing for about fifteen years and had won many national titles.

From Tony, I learned not only how to dance but also about

the dance world and lives of the other dance teachers I saw practicing every week. Some were top-ranked professionals in the ballroom world, and their skill was astonishing. Why, I wondered, were they teaching the likes of me how to foxtrot?

The not-so-glamorous reality is that being a world-class dancer, even a world champion, barely pays the bills. In order to subsidize their professional careers, the dancers often have to work at least one other job. They usually teach amateurs at independent studios like Pierre Dulaine or chain studios, such as Arthur Murray or Fred Astaire, and they often earn additional money by competing with their students in "Pro-Am" competitions. Some dancers are also costume designers, creating the elaborate gowns and striking men's dancewear the competition circuit demands, or they do hair and makeup at the competitions. Sometimes they work part-time jobs outside the ballroom world.

While Tony and I were dancing, he was focused on teaching me steps and "figures," which are a series of steps. After a few lessons with him I felt more comfortable and less awkward and self-conscious. We must have been quite a sight—Tony, tall and perfectly proportioned, and me, four foot ten and heavyset, with hair cropped shorter than his, and a face highlighted by chunky, black-framed glasses. Despite the difference in our statures, we moved gracefully together.

It's no secret that dancing is a very intimate act—you are held closely in the arms of your partner, and he leads you through the dance with his fingertips, hands, arms, hips, thighs, and feet. If he needs to change direction or adjust the routine in order to navigate the dance floor, you feel it without his having to say anything. That wordless communication takes place every moment when you're partner dancing. Having long been a teacher, Tony naturally was accustomed to the closeness of partner dancing. For me it was a rare blissful hour not only of movement but also of touch. It wasn't exactly sexual but it was sensual, and a buzz of sexuality was always in the air.

I hadn't focused on my body that intently for years; if anything, I had purposely ignored it once I knew that I might not be having sex for a very long time. They say your body holds sense memories, and as I danced with Tony my old self came flooding back—memories of Assad when he was well, of Hawaii, of all the ways I used to move and feel.

~

They say your body holds sense memories, and as I danced with Tony my old self came flooding back— memories of Assad when he was well, of Hawaii, of all the ways I used to move and feel.

~

After six months of dance lessons, I had my last coaching session with Suzanne. "I'm so grateful to you for leading me to ballroom dancing," I told her. By then my lessons were easily the highlight of my week, and within a year I would be describing ballroom dancing as a passion. I had never had a hobby before. I had poured all my effort and creativity into work. Now that I had found something I loved doing as much as public relations, I knew I would have to be more efficient with my energy so I could accommodate both passions. Yet as physically demanding as dancing was for me, it actually seemed to give me extra energy for the other areas of my life. I mulled this over with Suzanne at our final session.

"Here's my theory," I said. "No matter how dedicated and driven you are, and no matter how successful you've become, there comes a time in your career when you're going to hit a wall. Maybe you're overextended, taking care of family and work and everyone but yourself. Or something traumatic might have happened, like 9/11, which shakes up your view of the world. Maybe you're just burned out on the job. But you hit a wall, and the usual advice is to change jobs or positions within the company, or retrain for a new career. Instead, the solution might be to learn something that has nothing to do with your job or everyday life. Something you have no experience in, that's completely outside your comfort zone. And ideally it should be something physical so you have no choice but to be fully present and paying attention every second."

"You mean like tapping into the flow?" Suzanne asked. I knew what she was talking about—the state people achieve when they're creating, when the mind focuses on a task and the rest of the world slips away. It can happen any time you concentrate fully and become one with the activity, whether you're cooking or gardening or fixing a bicycle.

"That's different," I said. "For me, painting or hiking wouldn't work. I'd just keep thinking about the job or my other problems. I'd be multitasking again. It's as if every atom of my mind and body must be fully engaged. Only then can I really experience a total respite from my job, and the total respite is what revitalizes me."

⁓

"It's as if every atom of my mind and body must be fully engaged. Only then can I really experience a total respite from my job, and the total respite is what revitalizes me."

⁓

Although I had only been dancing a short while, one thing had already become clear. I always felt invigorated the day after a lesson. I had more energy for work and more patience when caring for Assad. I thought it might be the serotonin that was released from all that aerobic exercise, and no doubt that was part of it. But I had taken plenty of exercise classes, and they had never affected me this way. In addition to being fun and reconnecting me with parts of myself that

I had feared were gone forever—my youth, my femininity, and my childhood dreams—dancing engaged me because it was an entirely new domain. It wasn't something that came naturally to me, or that I could execute effortlessly, like PR. I couldn't coast the way I could in the bland routine of an aerobics class. My mind couldn't wander, or I would lose my balance and end up on the floor (yep—that happened). Ballroom dance was a totally new world, where I had to learn not only the moves but also the territory and the language, and do this in tandem with a partner. After all those years, I finally was learning how Ginger must have felt following Fred Astaire around the dance floor.

Over the first several months I was dancing with Tony, he schooled me on the complicated rules and categories of ballroom dance. There are two main styles, American and International. Only in the United States are both styles danced; most of the rest of the world dance the International style exclusively. Each style has its own version of dances that fall into two categories: International Standard and American Smooth dances, and International Latin and American Rhythm dances.

The standard/smooth dances include the waltz, tango, foxtrot, and Viennese waltz. An additional dance, the quickstep, is part of the standard repertoire only. These dances progress around the dance floor via a line of dance, a counterclockwise rotation around the room. The male partner negotiates the line of dance, navigating around the other couples on the floor. Standard is a rather formal, technical style that allows only closed dance positions, meaning positions where the partners stand very close together, facing each other, with their bodies parallel. Both hands have to be in contact with the partner's body at all times. In contrast, American Smooth style allows open and separated positions. Partners can be connected by only one hand and sometimes not connected at all, and they don't have to remain in close contact or parallel to each other throughout the dance. Overall, smooth is a freer style of dance that allows for far more individual expression. This is the style Tony dances, and what he was teaching me.

In International Latin and American Rhythm dances, the partners don't move around the dance floor as much as in standard and smooth but stay in a limited area. Some of these dances, such as the jive and the paso doble, are exclusive to International style. Some, like the East Coast swing, bolero, and mambo, are exclusive to American style. And there are a few crossover dances performed by American- and International-style dancers, like the cha cha, rumba, and samba, which are danced to similar music but with differing patterns and styling.

This simplified explanation of ballroom dancing is the tip of an iceberg of rules, steps, figures, routines, syllabi, categories, and skill levels (Bronze, Silver, and Gold) codified by the International DanceSport Federation, which governs all amateur, pro-am (where a professional dances with an amateur), and professional ballroom dance competitions. DanceSport was a name invented in the 1980s in an effort to position competitive ballroom dance as an Olympic sport (as of the 2008

Olympics, it had not been invited to join). It was intended to differentiate competitive partner dancing from social dancing, which took place in dance clubs, and from exhibition dancing, where professional dancers performed before an audience—on a cruise ship, for instance, or in a Broadway show.

I was intrigued when Tony told me that Fred and Ginger's famous dance club sequences actually bore a resemblance to the dancing done in clubs and dance halls of the 1910s–1940s. During that era, professionals were hired to perform at the clubs so patrons could see the latest dances and learn the steps. In 1920 Arthur Murray brought dance to the average citizen when he began publishing mail-order lessons. He launched his popular chain of dance studios in 1938. In 1947 Fred Astaire opened his own studio on Park Avenue in New York. Fred Astaire Dance Studios became a nationwide chain that, like Arthur Murray Dance Studios, continues to flourish today.

Arthur Murray, Fred Astaire, and other studios marketed dance not only as a healthy activity but also as a way to ascend the social ladder: if you knew the proper steps, you could dance alongside the Rockefellers and fit right in. Murray's mail-order lessons included not just the famous paper footprints (large sheets of paper with footprints in the pattern of specific dance steps, which students could place on the floor and follow), but also tips on manners and etiquette. For the World War II generation, knowing how to foxtrot and waltz became a valuable social skill, which they made sure their children learned as well.

The popularity of dance studios and partner dancing began to wane in the 1950s. By the 1970s ballroom dances were widely seen as throwbacks to another era, useful to know for weddings and not much else. But for some people, partner dancing retained its allure, and the dance industry adjusted to appeal to those who were still drawn to the glamour. The 1980s saw a rise in the popularity of ballroom dance, as it provided newly wealthy baby Boomers with a fun and extravagant pastime. While dance lessons didn't have to be expensive, there was no limit to how much you could spend on private teachers, fabulous gowns, and travel to competitions if you had the money and were bitten by the bug.

Ballroom dancing slowly started regaining momentum. In 1992 Baz Luhrmann directed an Australian film about competitive dancing called *Strictly Ballroom*, which became popular on the independent film circuit and was eventually screened in eighty-six countries. Then, in 1996, the Japanese movie *Shall We Dance* became an international hit. This sweet, critically acclaimed film told the story of a staid, conservative businessman going through a midlife crisis who conceals from his wife the fact that he is taking ballroom dance lessons. The film got my attention because of its Japanese cast. Prior to that I had only seen images of WASPs as ballroom dancers. (The American remake of *Shall We Dance*, which starred Richard Gere and Jennifer Lopez, didn't fare as well as the Japanese film. I don't think the premise of an American businessman secretly taking dance lessons was as great a cultural shock as it was in the much more reserved Japanese culture.)

The real breakthrough in public awareness of ballroom dancing would come in 2004, when the BBC retooled *Come*

Dancing, a long-running show about competitive ballroom dance, as *Strictly Come Dancing,* a show where celebrities were partnered with professional dancers and competed against one another. In 2006 ABC would launch an American version, *Dancing with the Stars,* and ballroom dancing would explode.

———

The siren call of Fred Astaire and Ginger Rogers had also bewitched many of the other dancers I met at the studio, professionals and amateurs alike. To this day, many consider Fred and Ginger to still be the gold standard of class, style, and skill when it comes to partner dancing. It's those two we are thinking of when we step onto the dance floor in our Technicolor ballroom world.

———

The musicals I had loved growing up were half a century old by the time I took my first dance lesson in 2002. Yet I discovered that the siren call of Fred Astaire and Ginger Rogers had also bewitched many of the other dancers I met at the studio, professionals and amateurs alike. To this day, many consider Fred and Ginger to still be the gold standard of class, style, and skill when it comes to partner dancing. It's those two we are thinking of when we step onto the dance floor in our Technicolor ballroom world.

The romantic image in my head of Fred and Ginger was accompanied by another: the fantasy that I could swirl around the dance floor in the arms of my very own tall, dark, and handsome prince, Assad. Unlike the *Shall We Dance* character John Clark (Shohei Sugiyama in the Japanese version), I was not holding out on my husband at all. My Arabian prince knew all about my ballroom dance lessons. In fact, not too long after I'd begun dancing, Assad and I took some group ballroom classes together. Assad's willingness to do this was no small thing given that he grew up in a very religious Muslim household where dance was strictly forbidden. We ultimately decided after a few frustrating attempts at the foxtrot that ballroom dance was my passion, not his. Assad was just happy that I had finally found a hobby—something that I'd never had before—and one that brought me such joy.

♪

My dance lessons were fun, but because I only took one lesson a week my progress was slow. Tony knew that in order to really improve, I should be taking more lessons. I hesitated, not yet willing to allow myself more than one hour a week of pure diversion. One day Tony casually said, "You know, with some more practice I'll bet you could dance a showcase."

"What's a showcase?"

"It's a dance recital at the studio where students perform for their friends and family."

I laughed out loud. "I'm not dancing in public. That's ridiculous!" But when I got home and told Assad about the idea, he was all for it. "You should do it," he said excitedly. "Then we can all come and watch you perform." *Great! That's just what I don't want*, I groaned inwardly.

The thought of dancing in public, even if it was just for friends and family, was terrifying. I was not a performer—not at all. I could make a presentation to a client, I could pitch a new business prospect, and I could deliver a speech to my colleagues in the PR industry, but that was hardly the same thing as waltzing around a dance studio in a ballroom gown and high heels. But Tony kept asking me about it, and one day he sweetened the deal with an offer I couldn't refuse. "I'll choreograph a special samba routine for you if you'll do the showcase."

I had nagged Tony to teach me the samba as soon as we started dancing together, so his offer to choreograph a samba routine made me momentarily forget my fear of having to perform it in front of an audience. My whole body responded viscerally to samba music, which I had loved even before I knew it was samba. It's the bounce in the music that makes dancing the samba so joyful.

Samba is considered the most difficult of the rhythm and Latin dances. Not only is it fast but producing a proper "samba bounce action" requires coordinating pushes, ticks, and circles from foot to ankle to knee to pelvis to hip. Some dancers accentuate the distinctive pelvic tick with abdominal crunching. The tick initiates a figure-eight motion of the hips. If it's below your rib cage, you're working it when you samba!

So many moving parts to the samba, but I *loved* this dance of celebration and joy! Tony's offer to choreograph an entire samba routine for me was irresistible.

Once I agreed to do the samba showcase, I increased my dance lessons to three times a week. That's when my partners at PT&Co. started to get nervous. Business was still very dicey, and although the agency was a collective, I was the one in charge. The stress of running a collective was one more thing that had begun to wear me down. It had been a long, exhilarating road, but after twelve years I was tired of trying to get consensus on all the main issues while also satisfying my powerful alpha urge to control every detail.

Patrice Tanaka & Company Inc. (or PT&Co. as we were also known) was founded in 1990, when I led a buyback of our PR agency from the advertising behemoth Chiat/Day, our then-parent company. Chiat/Day was a creative powerhouse—and borderline sweatshop—named "Agency of the Decade" by *Advertising Age* and nicknamed "Chiat/Day and night" by its overworked and stressed-out employees. The small PR agency where I worked, Jessica Dee Communications (which I helped the owner grow from a four- to a twenty-person shop), was acquired by Chiat/Day in 1987. Jay Chiat, the agency's visionary founder, had the idea of providing clients with all marketing services under one agency umbrella, or as he referred to it, "the whole egg concept." Our agency was acquired to provide Chiat/Day clients with PR support. Two years into our acquisition, founder Jessica Dee resigned and I was left running our PR subsidiary.

By 1989 I was managing a team of twenty-five talented, creative, and sometimes eccentric PR pros, and we had produced our most successful campaign to date, for Korbel Champagne. It began with a simple ad we placed in the classified section of the *Wall Street Journal*: "Wanted: Director of Romance." The idea that such a corporate job actually existed captured people's imaginations and garnered huge publicity, as well as more than twelve hundred resumes from lawyers, bankers, CFOs, and other executives desperate for a little romance in their lives. The Director of Romance was one of two positions we filled in creating corporate America's first-ever "Department of Romance, Weddings & Entertaining"—all of the occasions people celebrate with champagne. This campaign, which we ran for four years, ultimately resulted in a 50 percent growth of Korbel Champagne sales during a period when the overall champagne/sparkling wine category actually declined 12 percent.

Our romance with Korbel ended when the company decided to consolidate its PR and advertising under one roof—and it wasn't Chiat/Day's. It was early 1990 and the money train of the roaring eighties was beginning to lose steam. Budgets were tightening, even at Chiat/Day. I knew that when I told management we had lost our biggest client, they would make me fire the four members of our team who had worked nearly full-time on the brand. If I did so, we wouldn't have the talent or expertise we would need to replace those lost billings. I started wracking my brain for a way to keep the team intact, and the only solution I could think of was to buy back the agency from Chiat/Day so that I could have control over firing and hiring decisions.

There were several problems with this plan. First, I had no idea how to go about it. Second, we had no money. Third, not everyone on my team wanted to break off from the hottest ad agency in America. I spent the next few months in meetings with the eleven key individuals at our PR agency, painting a picture of what would happen if the economy went into a recession, something many of our clients said was inevitable. I told my colleagues that Chiat/Day would likely decide to batten down the hatches and focus on its core business of advertising. That meant the company would either shut down or sell off all of its subsidiary operations, including us. With the worsening economy, I proposed we not just sit around waiting for the other shoe to drop but instead proactively approach Chiat/Day about letting us buy back our agency. After weeks of meetings, I finally got a majority of my eleven key colleagues to agree. Now all I had to do was persuade Jay Chiat.

Bronx-born, blunt, and obsessed with pushing the advertising envelope, Jay was the undisputed creative giant of the era. He demanded fierce loyalty from his employees and could be brutal and petty if displeased. I carefully planned my approach, calculating that he might be in a more generous mood if I called him while he was attending the International Design Conference in Aspen, Colorado. I had attended this gathering the previous year with Jay and my ex-boss, Jessica, so I knew that Jay would probably be in a relaxed and expansive mood. This future-focused conference, where intellectuals opined on design as a strategic force in improving business and enhancing global prosperity, was a tonic to Mr. Chiat. I waited until he was in Aspen for a couple of days, and then I started calling him. When he finally returned my fifth call, I launched into a heartfelt speech about how unhappy we were at Chiat/Day because, as PR practitioners, we were treated as second-class citizens within the advertising agency. I asked him if he would please let us buy the agency back so that we could focus on doing great PR, which was the reason Chiat/Day had acquired us. After a very long pause he said, "If you're saying that you all want to do this, I guess we'll have to come to some accommodation."

"Jay, thank you so much. I really appreciate—" *click*. He hung up on me.

Chiat/Day wanted one million dollars for our PR subsidiary. We didn't have it. We finally arranged a deal where two colleagues and I would turn in our Chiat/Day stock and also give Chiat/Day a royalty on our revenues for the next three years. PT&Co., an employee-owned PR agency, was born in July 1990. A few months later, I hired Evelyn Calleja, our controller, putting our agency at thirteen employees.

In retrospect, I'm not sure I would again form a company with twelve other co-owners and operate it with a consensus-style management, but at the time it felt like the right thing to do. When I was growing up, my mother always told me, "Share your cookies and toys." It seemed to me that if I was asking people to start a new company just when the economy was heading south, sharing the risk and potential reward made sense. Ed Lipton, the lawyer I hired to negotiate the deal, disagreed vehemently. In fact, he begged me not to do it. "It's difficult enough for any new business to succeed, even with just one owner," he warned. "The problems are magnified if you have two owners. But twelve owners? That is just insane!"

—

When I was growing up, my mother always told me, "Share your cookies and toys." It seemed to me that if I was asking people to start a new company just when the economy was heading south, sharing the risk and potential reward made sense.

—

He was wrong. It worked, but it was not easy. What I didn't think about at the time was that everybody was at a different stage in their lives, professionally and personally. We ranged across the age spectrum from midtwenties to midforties, and our employee-owners' level of maturity reflected that. While many of us understood that having our own business meant having to work even harder, others thought it meant that as an "owner" you were entitled to work less and to decide for yourself what you would or would not do. The group decision-making process could be excruciatingly slow. It took years just to develop a shareholders' agreement. A lot of time was spent defining our responsibilities and authority as "owners"—time that could have been focused on growing our agency.

Yet in the end, thirteen people with thirteen different perspectives created not only a successful public relations agency but a family-friendly workplace that embodied the values upon which we all agreed. At the core of our philosophy was the belief that, if we took care of our employee-owners, they would, in turn, look after our clients in this service-oriented business. PT&Co. was a "workplace community" committed to working together and supporting one another. Moreover, as a workplace community, we believed that our agency had an obligation to contribute in a positive way to the greater community in which we operated.

This sense of PT&Co. as a workplace community was put to its first test during the recession of 1990–91. We didn't know it at the time but July 1990, when we started the agency, was the official start of that recession. Within six months of buying back the agency, we lost half our billings. When that happens, the prudent response is for the agency to reduce its staff accordingly. I knew, however, that if we laid off half of our employee-owners, it would just be a matter of months before everyone else abandoned ship. There was only one way forward: no one should be let go, everyone should take a pay cut, and we should all redouble our efforts to build the agency. And that's what we did.

Twelve months later, lifted by a recovering economy, PT&Co. had grown 100 percent and we were back to the amount of billings we had when we started the agency, without having lost any employees. In the process, we gained the knowledge that even in the worst of times we would not abandon one another. Instead, we would support one another and protect our workplace community. Together, we carved out a niche for PT&Co. as an agency committed to creating great work (because that's what attracts and keeps clients), a great workplace (because that's what attracts and retains top talent), and great communities that work, meaning healthy, sustainable communities (because we wanted to contribute in a positive way to making the world a better place). By the mid-1990s we were winning prestigious clients and dozens of awards, including two I treasure the most: "#1 Most Creative Agency," awarded in 1997 by the *Holmes Report,* a major PR industry trade media outlet, and the "#2 Best Workplace" among all PR agencies in America.

When the economy started to shrink again in 2000 with the dot-com bust, we weren't immediately affected because we didn't have a heavy base of technology clients. We felt more than strong enough to weather a slight dip in business. By 2002, that confidence had been shaken by the one-two punch of the 2001 recession and the terrorist attacks on 9/11. So when I started disappearing at 6 p.m. sharp, or in the middle of the workday to go to a dance lesson, it set off alarms for my partners. One afternoon, as I was about to leave, Ellen popped into my office waving a document.

"Aren't you going to edit this memo?" she asked me.

"No."

"Did you look at it?"

"Yes. I think it's terrific."

"You didn't even look at it."

"Yes I did."

"Where's the red ink? Where are your edits?"

"No edits. We've worked together for fifteen years. I've decided to finally trust you," I joked. It was true. And now that I was preparing for my samba showcase, I had neither the time nor the inclination to pick through every piece of copy, tweaking it until it was exactly the way I wanted. Something had to give.

"Hmmm," said Ellen, and left my office looking worried.

I hadn't confided to my partners how depressed I had been before I started taking dance lessons. It would only have added to their anxiety. I alone knew that dancing wasn't a hobby, it was a life raft. Reclaiming my life was a conscious act that required scheduling time for me on a regular basis. In order to stay effective and creative at PT&Co., supportive of Assad, and excited about the future, I needed to be as committed to myself as I had always been to my work, my husband, and all my other obligations. Right now that meant dance lessons three times a week.

—

Dancing wasn't a hobby, it was a life raft. Reclaiming my life was a conscious act that required scheduling time for me on a regular basis.

—

I'll always be grateful to my executive coach, Suzanne, for asking me, "What is your purpose? What brings you joy?" When I blurted out "Dancing!" little did I know that it would lead to a lifelong passion, or that the lessons I learned on the ballroom floor would help me guide PT&Co. through its most turbulent years.

INTERMEZZO

Foxtrot

EVERY BALLROOM DANCE has its own distinct essence and attitude. Former ballroom champion Marianne Nicole believes that people's personalities match certain dances: romantic (bolero), joyful (samba), or perhaps just plain difficult (mambo, because no one listens to the "one" beat). If that's true, then foxtrot's personality would be breezy. When the nervous newcomer stands awkwardly on the dance floor, feeling shy as a kindergartner and just as knobby-kneed, the instructor can be confident that within a few lessons even the most hesitant student will be able to master the foxtrot's basic moves.

Sauntering across the floor, the foxtrot embodies the saucy coolness we associate with Fred Astaire and Ginger Rogers when they're taking it easy to a Cole Porter or Irving Berlin tune. Many a wedding couple has made its debut as Mr. and Mrs. with a simple but charming foxtrot. Why foxtrot? Because in its most basic form the foxtrot teaches two of the foundational skills of smooth dances: standing up straight and walking in harmony with a partner. If you can walk, you can foxtrot. And if you can abandon the Hunchback of Notre Laptop look, you can also appear elegant doing it.

Most of the patterns of foxtrot follow a slow-slow-quick-quick rhythm, and, just as in walking, you never have to worry which foot goes next, a question that panics nearly every beginner. If you are leader, it's always left, right, left, right, and so on. For follower, it's always right, left, right, left. (As Ginger Rogers noted, she had to do everything Fred did, only backward and in heels.) In the basic foxtrot step, the leader takes a long, slow stride forward with the left foot, then another slow forward step with the right foot, then a quick side step with the left foot, followed by the right foot quickly closing to the left foot. Forward, forward, side, together. The follower walks in a mirror image with a slow stride back on the right foot, another back on the left, then a quick side step with the right foot, followed by the left foot quickly closing to the right foot. Back, back, side, together.

Walking in harmony, even with a beloved, takes coordination and sensitivity. That's why it's a dance, not a pleasant stroll. One of the key ways to indicate movement or direction is through frame, which is the shape and connection of the leader's and follower's shoulders, arms, and hands.

Many observers of ballroom dance like to say, "The man is the frame and the woman is the beautiful picture," but frame is an equal responsibility for the partners. The leader is not holding the follower up and out with the strength of his arms. The follower holds up her own arms. The leader is not using frame to push and pull the follower to the right place. The follower receives the signal initiated from the leader's frame and then puts herself there. The leader cannot move more than the amount of space the follower opens up for him. Without cooperation, the couple is not going anywhere!

Since foxtrot does not make big demands of speed or sway from the beginner, it's also an ideal dance for learning how to have a good frame with your partner. You will move as one and not look like you're squabbling your way across life's speed bumps, arguing, "I'm the boss," "No, I'm the boss!"

Foxtrot teaches you how to relax and enjoy the benefits of teamwork on the dance floor. If you're moving backward, you can enjoy the reassurance of a partner who can see where you're going and will protect your interests. If you're moving forward, you can appreciate the generosity of a partner who responds to your every motion with keen attentiveness. The sheer harmony of partner dancing will have you humming Frank Sinatra-style, "Heaven, I'm in heaven, and my heart beats so that I can hardly speak, and I seem to find the happiness I seek, when we're out together dancing cheek to cheek."

CHAPTER 4

Samba Girl

"Stifling an urge to dance is bad for your
health—it rusts your spirit and your hips."

—Terri Guillemets

*M*y dance teacher, Tony, still gets a kick out of reminding me that I'm the only student who ever called him at home on the day of a showcase asking to go over the routine one last time—verbally.

"Just talk me through that part I always screw up," I begged him. So Tony talked me through the sequence of steps as he drove his wife, Susan, to the mall that Saturday morning. I was a nervous wreck. I couldn't believe I had agreed to do the showcase, and as the event got closer, three lessons a week were not enough to convince me that I would be prepared. I went over the samba routine in my head obsessively, terrified that I would forget a step, throw the whole thing off, and embarrass myself.

I had been getting more and more nervous as the big day approached. *Why am I putting myself in a situation to perform a dance in front of perfect strangers? Have I lost my mind?* But I kept showing up for lessons and practicing my routine. On a business trip to San Francisco, I found what I thought was a perfect samba dress at Neiman Marcus. Black, of course, because I still wanted to camouflage my body.

The showcase took place in the evening at Pierre Dulaine's studio. Chairs lined three walls of the dance floor, lending the room a festive, expectant air that reminded me of the last place I had seen this: at a friend's ballet recital when

I was five years old. My private cheering section—Assad; my partners, Evelyn and Frank; my assistant, Maureen "Mo" Stammers, who had begged to attend; and another close friend, Brenda Fields—were sitting together talking and laughing, waiting for the showcase to begin. The buzz of the audience only fueled my buzz of stage fright.

Finally Pierre Dulaine, dressed formally in a tuxedo, walked onto the dance floor and graciously welcomed everyone. He thanked them for coming and told the guests how hard the students and teachers had worked to present the evening's showcase. I was with Tony and other students performing that evening, waiting nervously and unseen by the audience in a corridor that ran parallel to the ballroom. As each couple's turn came, Pierre would announce the student, the teacher, and the dance they would be performing. Pierre operated the music system that evening, making sure the correct CD was played for every performance. Otto Cappel, his partner and manager of the studio, videotaped the dancers so we would each have a record of our performance. A female professional dancer I didn't know had been hired to judge the showcase, not to score our performances but to give each student some brief, written feedback. She sat at a little table right next to my private cheering section.

When we heard the opening bars of our samba, Tony took my hand and escorted me onto the dance floor. The samba beat delivered its usual magic, lifting my spirits and pulling me into its rhythm. Tony and I swung into our routine, moving around the ballroom as if we had done it hundreds of times before, which we probably had. It all went smoothly until we came to the section I had called Tony about that morning. Sure enough, I flubbed it, but Tony gracefully twirled me into the next move and the rest of the routine proceeded without a hitch. At times it seemed like our ninety-second samba went on forever, but it also seemed to be over in a flash.

As soon as we ended the dance, Tony guided me across the floor to curtsy in front of the judge. Up jumped Assad and our friends, each bearing a sign with a "10" written on it like at an Olympic event, to give me a perfect total score of fifty. As the judge and the audience laughed, I turned to give my personal cheering section a formal curtsy.

Just before the showcase began, Tony had told me not to worry because "nobody knows who you are." *He's right,* I thought. *New York is a big town. It doesn't matter if I screw up; I don't know any of these people.* That calmed me down and I went onto the dance floor a little less stressed. Now, as we headed to our chairs, a woman approached me with a big smile on her face.

"Aren't you Patrice Tanaka, president of New York Women in Communications?" she asked. Inwardly I cringed. I was indeed president of NYWICI that year—not exactly an obscure position, as the group organized an annual gala honoring the nation's top women in all fields of communications that took place in the packed Grand Ballroom of the Waldorf-Astoria. So much for New York being a big anonymous town. This NYWICI "sister" was surprised and excited to see me among the performers and gushed over my dancing. The cringing made way for some inward glowing: I felt like a star!

After the showcase and our celebration dinner at Sushi Samba—an aptly named place—I went home to look at the video of my performance. Assad kissed me and went off to bed, very proud of me. I stayed up and watched my video over and over. I just could not believe I had actually performed a dance in front of strangers. For months after the showcase I would watch the video, still not believing that it was me performing a samba! It was truly one of the most thrilling things I had ever done.

My dancing in the showcase was not great, but I felt great doing it. It gave me such a rush that I couldn't wait to dance the next showcase. I was crestfallen to learn that Pierre held them only twice a year.

"I can't wait another six months," I whined to Tony.

"Well, we could compete in a small dance competition here in the city next month," he suggested.

I was so excited about performing again that I immediately agreed to compete in the New York Dance Festival. I totally forgot about my self-consciousness and the gut-wrenching terror of performing in front of an audience. I just wanted to feel the pure adrenaline rush of dancing the showcase and, afterward, to relive that exquisite moment again and again while watching the video. I wanted to feel that sense of accomplishment and wonderment that I had done something so unlike my everyday me. If my goal was to feel joy, this was the way to do it.

⌒

*I just wanted to feel the pure
adrenaline rush of dancing the
showcase and, afterward, to relive that
exquisite moment again and again
while watching the video. I wanted
to feel that sense of accomplishment
and wonderment that I had done
something so unlike my everyday me.*

⌒

Some years later, I read a passage in Elizabeth Gilbert's *Eat, Pray, Love* that perfectly described what I was feeling at that time: "To devote yourself to the creation and enjoyment of beauty, then, can be a serious business—not always necessarily a means of escaping reality, but sometimes a means of holding on to the real when everything else is flaking away." My femininity, creativity, and optimism had been flaking away, especially since 9/11. When I was dancing, I felt real and complete again. For the first time in fifteen years, I had something to counterbalance my focus on work and Assad. Dancing was something I did just for me—not shareholders or clients or friends or husband. Bringing joy back into my

Photo by Albert Parker, Parker West Photography

Me dancing rhythm with Tony Scheppler at my first ballroom competition. My initial nerves evaporated into pure joy. Can you tell?

life was serious business. And as I had told Suzanne, dancing actually made me more energetic and productive at work. The ironic aspect of this revelation was that I had always believed in and promoted a balance between life and work. Our agency was based on that model. It's just that I had never applied it to myself.

It was in the salt mines of Chiat/Day that I first understood how counterproductive all work and no break could be to employee morale and creativity. Not only in advertising and PR, but in most industries, there is a macho work ethic that rewards people for powering though fatigue. Chiat/Day encouraged a manic one-upmanship of overwork that was hard to resist. An ongoing joke was, "If you don't come in on Saturday, don't bother coming in on Sunday." It wasn't uncommon for people to spend twenty-four hours at the office, having all-night brainstorming sessions to come up with another campaign concept because the client hated what was presented that day, or rewriting copy over and over. The creative results of a caffeine-fueled, twenty-hour work marathon weren't always brilliant. Sometimes they reminded me of the genius ideas you wake up with at 2 a.m. If you manage to scrawl them down on a notepad, in the morning they often turn out to be indecipherable, weird, or just hackneyed. When we started PT&Co., I wanted to make sure we didn't get sucked into that type of unproductive and exhausting work mentality.

To change that culture, we would have to do something proactive. We would need to establish policies that supported balance while recognizing the reality that if you want to stay competitive in PR, you sometimes have to work very long hours. Ideally, our office would have a quiet, relaxing space where people could go to escape the pressure during those intense periods of work.

Four years after starting the agency, we got that place of refuge. When we needed to move to a bigger office in 1994, I had something very specific in mind—an airy, sunlit, loft-like space with windows on three sides. When one of my partners found the seventh floor of a renovated, mixed-use commercial building in the West Village and brought me to see it, I instantly shouted, "This is it!" After we signed the lease, another partner, John Frazier, asked me how I envisioned the office layout. John, who was extremely organized, meticulous, and possessed a strong sense of design, would be working with the contractor/designer to build out our space. I told him I wanted an open floor plan with low-rise cubicles. There would be none of the traditional senior-executive offices lining the perimeter of the floor and hogging all the light. I also wanted our office to honor the total needs of employees to work, eat, and relax: "In addition to workspaces and meeting rooms, let's have a living room, a kitchen, a dining area, and a meditation room."

I was intent on having a meditation room not only to enable people to take breaks from work but also to institutionalize respite as part of the culture at PT&Co. It's one thing to tell people, "Go ahead, take a break." But if the only place they can take it is at their desks or in a noisy lunchroom, how valuable is that break? A meditation room would signal to our staff that we really meant it—at our agency, break time was considered a vital part of the creative process. It was also an acknowledgment that in order to do great work, we would sometimes have to come in early, stay late, and spend more time at the office than any of us would prefer. If that was the case, I wanted our co-owners and staff always to have a beautiful, comfortable, quiet space where they could retreat.

We used the meditation room for yoga sessions, group meditation sessions, belly dance classes, and other nonwork pursuits. Everyone understood right away that an hour in the meditation room was more restorative than, for example, an hour in our lunchroom. At lunch we would inevitably talk about work or personal problems; our pace didn't really change. But in the meditation room we were consciously doing something that was not work. It was a true break for both body and mind, and that is what reenergized us. Given the passionate debates, the pressure, and the long hours that were unavoidable in public relations, the meditation room ended up being some of the most valuable square footage in the office.

Why is PR so demanding? First and foremost, it is a service business. We have clients to serve and, more important, to surprise and delight. Like most competitive business enterprises, PR agencies attract and retain clients by coming up with creative solutions to their marketing and business challenges. This process requires a lot of time and energy for critical thinking, brainstorming, and implementation, as well as perseverance in the face of obstacles and, oftentimes, shifting priorities and parameters of the assignment. All of this work needs to be done on tight deadlines. If you win an account, the pressure only intensifies in trying to satisfy and delight the client so you can retain and grow their business. And with the explosion of online and social media, there is never-ending work to feed the beast of a twenty-four hour, global news-and-information cycle.

This is especially true when a campaign features a big event, like the Dyson launch at Fashion Week. PR campaigns for major new product introductions often involve staging an unusual or extravagant event in order to attract the attention of key media and influencers and, in turn, reach target customers and consumers. Our agency has staged many high-profile events in New York, including the fifteenth anniversary of the "I Love New York" campaign; the fiftieth anniversary of Circle Line Sightseeing Yachts (involving a flotilla of boats and a fireworks display on the Hudson River); the 125th anniversary of Spiegel Catalog (featuring a black-tie gala event at the Metropolitan Museum of Art and a surprise performance by Liza Minnelli); and the consumer launch of Microsoft's Windows 95 (where we created a three-tent venue at Lincoln Center for the media event and also lit up the Empire State Building in the brand's colors). Whenever we staged an event, it was all hands on deck to make sure it was a success.

In the case of Dyson, we piggybacked the U.S. introduction of the vacuum cleaner onto Fashion Week, which was already a media magnet. Combining Dyson with Fashion Week was an efficient way to capture the attention of the fifty thousand influencers that flocked to the tents twice a year. But we also created event venues from scratch, like we did three years later when Dyson introduced the DC15 upright vacuum, known as "The Ball." To reinforce Dyson's reputation for innovation, we erected a ninety-foot inflatable yellow ball in midtown Manhattan, highlighting the unique feature of this vacuum that made maneuverability a breeze. The attention-getting yellow sphere, which we used for the consumer and trade launch events, contained interactive displays, a 3-D presentation of the DC15, and an obstacle course allowing visitors to test-drive the new vacuum.

We welcomed any opportunity to align our client's brand with a beloved institution, like when we took over Manhattan's huge upscale toy store, FAO Schwarz, to promote Emeril Lagasse's line of cookware designed just for kids. It was the kind of event that could only have taken place in the food-crazed, cash-flush New York of the early 2000s. We had been working with Emeril for a few years as a result of one of our longest-running client relationships, a high-end cookware company named All-Clad. One of our early recommendations to All-Clad had been to equip the kitchen stage sets of the then-fledgling Food Network with the brand's distinctive-looking product. If the goal of public relations is to obtain a high amount of visibility at a fraction of the cost of advertising, this seemed like a terrific opportunity.

In the Food Network's early days, All-Clad was featured on most of the cooking shows, including *Essence of Emeril*. As Emeril's popularity grew, we suggested to All-Clad that it manufacture a signature pan for him. It did so, christening it the Emeril Everyday Pan. That year it was the best-selling piece of cookware in America. All-Clad then entered into a ten-year relationship with Emeril to create a complete line of cookware called Emerilware. Today nearly every celebrity chef has his or her own line of cookware, but the Emeril Everyday Pan is the granddaddy of them all.

One of All-Clad's challenges was to launch Emerilware without sabotaging potential sales for its costlier All-Clad line. Emerilware had to perform as well as All-Clad but look different and be more affordable. To achieve this, Emeril suggested specific touches that would make the cookware easy for people to use, such as little spouts on saucepans, riveted handles, and angled sides. Like the chef himself, Emerilware was accessible to the people. Emeril personally tested every piece of his cookware.

I have to take a moment here to mention how gracious and good-natured Emeril Lagasse was to everyone he met during our collaboration with him. At the annual International Home & Housewares Show in Chicago, where we would introduce his latest cookware to the trade, people would line up to have him autograph recipe cards we printed for the occasion. He'd spend a minute or two with each person, and had the ability to make every single one of them feel as if he or she were the center of the universe. He had an astonishing ability to remember people's names. Ellen LaNicca, who attended this annual trade show, told me that even though she only saw Emeril once a year he always knew her name.

In 2002 Emeril wrote his first cookbook for children, *There's a Chef in My Soup!* To accompany it, All-Clad launched a line of Emerilware for kids. The pans and utensils were sized for a child's hand but designed to cook real food. It was a natural extension of the foodie culture, and also a way for parents and kids to bond in the kitchen.

FAO Schwarz was the ideal place to launch the product. We staged the event as a big, fun party for New Yorkers and their kids—"Come on in, check out our new children's cookware and cookbook, and meet the author." A casual sort of event, except that this was Emeril, and we had barely opened the doors before hundreds of people pushed their way inside and started lining up to say *"Bam!"*—Emeril's signature exhortation—to the chef. Talk about pressure! Try entertaining a thousand eager parents and children waiting in line over the course of a few hours. We had magicians roaming the line, doing tricks. We had folks handing out balloons. We gave child-sized chef hats and aprons with *BAM!* printed on them to anyone who bought the cookware. There were staffers whose only job was to bring water to people waiting in line. There was an area where attendees could decorate cupcakes, and a booth where kids could get their faces painted. Everyone—adults, children, entertainers, the security guards, FAO Schwarz staff, and those of us at PT&Co.—had a fabulous time.

What I remember most about that day was how many people said *"BAM!"* to Emeril and how many asked him, "Can you give me a *'BAM'*?" Even if it was the five hundredth time, he would smile and look right at them and say, *"BAM!"* The man never tired. He completely grasped that these people waiting in line were his fans and he was successful because of them. Throughout the ten years we were lucky enough to work with Emeril, he remained an amazing marketing partner and consummate gentleman.

The Emerilware kids' cookware launch stands out in my mind as an event that, although high-pressure, was satisfying on every level—great client, lots of publicity, and a wonderful time for everyone. PT&Co. worked like a well-oiled machine that day. This isn't always the case. Sometimes, as soon as the outside pressure relents, the internal pressure ramps up.

Our co-owners, including me, were a fairly high-strung group of New York PR people, so it's not surprising that things could get emotionally messy at times. By 2001 there were six remaining partners, supported by a staff of forty. Seven original partners had left the agency—some left New York, and some left public relations altogether. Among the remaining partners, Frank de Falco was particularly excitable and sensitive. Along with Frank, Evelyn and I were probably the most emotional of the group. Maria Kalligeros amped up the anxiety by anticipating the worst, although she redeemed herself with an acidic and dead-on sense of humor. Ellen LaNicca, John Frazier, and Fran Kelly were more measured, but they still had their opinions about how the agency should be run and didn't hesitate to speak their minds.

Our draining shareholder meetings seemed to bring out the worst in all of us. Inevitably, some shareholders would express their feelings that they should have more authority, perks, recognition, shares in the company, higher salaries, titles, and so forth. Frank, Evelyn, and Ellen preferred that I be the leader and make the decisions. Maria, Fran, and John wanted to have more decision-making authority.

At one point, to try to address some of these issues, I made four of them "presidents," each heading their own practice. Frank thought it was ridiculous that our small agency had four presidents and suggested that we change our name to "Presidents 'R Us."

If only to have a place to get away from one another, we really needed that meditation room. Some people prayed in there. Some took naps. New mothers used it as a lactation room. I didn't care what employees used the meditation room for as long it helped them with whatever form of time-out they might need to get through the workday more gracefully. Also, in the meditation room, we could relate to one another as people, not simply coworkers.

⁓

Some people prayed in there. Some took naps. New mothers used it as a lactation room. I didn't care what employees used the meditation room for as long it helped them with whatever form of time-out they might need to get through the workday more gracefully.

⁓

Having this care-for-one-another's-soul approach at work fits with the community-building attitude I had cultivated—without knowing it!—ever since I had arrived in New York. Like the tropical décor in my home, creating community in a big, anonymous place like New York was my way of bringing the small-town feel of the Islands to Manhattan. For many people in New York, their primary community is their workplace. At PT&Co. we had not only the meditation room but also family-friendly policies and a one-for-all culture: when times were tight we all took salary cuts; layoffs were always the last resort.

It was with a community-building mindset that we started a Valentine's Day program in 1996 called "Acts of Love & Kindness." I wanted to expand the concept of love from "romantic love" to "brotherly love," so I suggested that we close the agency on Valentine's Day and give employees the day off to commit whatever loving act they chose. The following year, PT&Co. volunteered to organize a larger Valentine's Day effort on behalf of the Public Relations Society of America, New York chapter, involving thirty other PR agencies in the city. At its height, more than fifty agencies participated in the program.

Our commitment to the community at large evolved into one of PT&Co.'s most significant niches—cause-related marketing. My partners and I felt we should take on ethical clients and urge them to do PR campaigns that had a positive impact on society. We wanted to distinguish our agency from those that didn't care whether their clients were ethical, as long as they paid handsomely. We also knew that working on campaigns that had a positive impact on the community at large would attract the type of talented PR employees with whom we wanted to work.

Our longest-running cause-related campaign was launched shortly after we started PT&Co. In November 1991 a friend referred us to the late Wendy Banks, executive vice president of marketing at Liz Claiborne. This was exciting news for our fledgling agency, because a big national apparel brand like Liz Claiborne could help put us on the map. Wendy was an inspired marketer and a very intense, voluble woman. When we met with her, she got to the point quickly. Liz Claiborne, the designer, had made a name for herself in the 1970s by creating clothes for the working woman, which was a novel business proposition at the time. By 1991 Liz Claiborne, the company, was an aging brand that had lost its innovative edge. Nearly every apparel manufacturer was designing clothes for working women by then. Wendy was looking for a brand PR campaign that would help the company regain its pioneering edge and create a stronger emotional bond with its core customers.

"Whom do you consider your core consumers?" I asked her. "What age group?"

"Women ages sixteen to sixty," she said.

We almost fell off our chairs. I had never heard any marketer give such a wide age range for its core consumers.

As the conversation unfolded, Wendy set out a few parameters for our PR campaign. We had to achieve this new emotional bond with all women between the ages of sixteen and sixty without suggesting any changes to the brand's existing product lines, or creating any promotions that might inter-fere with store operations, either at the company's free-standing Liz Claiborne stores, or in the department stores selling its product lines. And it shouldn't cost too much.

Back at the office we considered our options, with the numbers "sixteen to sixty" still ringing in our ears. To create an emotional bond with the Liz Claiborne customers, we needed to address an issue that mattered deeply to them. One way to achieve this was through a cause-related marketing campaign that resonated with women. The question was, which cause would strike a chord with all those age groups?

To find out, we identified and researched about eighteen possible issues and causes that Liz Claiborne might embrace. A giant Excel spreadsheet captured the attributes and chal-lenges of each issue, such as the number of other national companies involved in the cause and the cost of entry (the minimum campaign budget needed to make an impact on the issue, given the number of companies already involved that were also trying to "own" it). We researched breast cancer (thirty national companies were already involved), educa-tion, the environment, AIDS and other diseases, hunger relief, and homelessness, to name a few.

The issue that emerged from our massive audit was domestic violence. This was not what we wanted to hear. How would a prospective client whom we barely knew react when we suggested that it champion such an unpretty issue, especially a fashion brand whose customers were depart-ment stores and other specialty retailers? Shopping was all about escapism, and it was hard to imagine retailers wanting to bring a downer of an issue like domestic violence into the shopping experience.

Yet everything pointed to our recommending a campaign that would raise awareness of domestic violence. Chief among the reasons was that there were no other national companies or brands involved, so Liz Claiborne could "own" the issue at a fairly low cost of entry. Additionally, by having the courage to take on such a gritty issue, Liz Claiborne could reclaim its pioneering heritage as a company willing to go where no company had gone before. It was a tremendous opportunity.

We were so nervous about making this recommendation that we commissioned even more research—a nationally projectable omnibus survey of about five hundred American women. We asked only two questions (because that's all we could afford for this new business pitch): Do you think domestic violence is a problem in America today? If you believe that domestic violence is a problem in America today, would you feel predisposed toward a company that tried to address this problem? The findings blew us away. The response to both questions was in the high 80- to low 90-percentile range. I was shocked because, at the time, domestic violence was very rarely covered by the media. Armed with this data, we prepared to recommend that Liz Claiborne launch a cause-related PR campaign focused on awareness and prevention of domestic violence.

What we didn't know until after our presentation was that Jerry Chazen, Liz Claiborne's then-CEO, was very much aware of the issue and that he and his wife, Simona, even funded a local women's shelter in West Nyack, New York. Jerry, who initially seemed a little bored with the idea of meeting with us, became more and more alert as the presentation went on. He and Wendy immediately approved the idea, which became the "Love Is Not Abuse" program that is still going strong today, nineteen years later. It's the longest-running corporate campaign addressing the issue of domestic violence. Much of the great work for this campaign, which won Liz Claiborne and our agency more than forty awards, was led for many years by my brilliant and talented colleague Maria Kalligeros. In 2010, our "Love Is Not Abuse" campaign was cited by the *Holmes Report* as one of the "Top Five PR Campaigns of the Decade."

A cause-related campaign can take many forms. For "Love Is Not Abuse" we produced billboards, radio and TV public service announcements, educational posters, handbooks, and brochures. The effort expanded to include campus workshops, employee education campaigns, fund-raising, charity shopping days, and much more. "Love Is Not Abuse" helped to reposition the issue of domestic violence from a shameful family secret to what it really was: a public health crisis—one out of every four American women has experienced domestic violence, as has one of three women globally.

By helping to bring the problem into the light of public awareness, the necessary resources were mobilized to address this crisis. The media, once silent on the topic, began to cover it regularly. Public outcry led to the passage of state and national laws protecting women. With the appropriate laws in place, judges could take action. Perhaps most important, the attitude of the police changed. In the past, they had often treated domestic violence as a family matter and declined to get involved. New laws mandated that they had to arrest offenders, even if the battered woman tried to "take back" her complaint, which was all too common.

The positive impact of Liz Claiborne's "Love Is Not Abuse" program was a beautiful example of the win-win aspect of cause-related campaigns. Liz Claiborne got long-term positive publicity (nearly two decades' worth) and reburnished its reputation as a pioneering brand. The campaign improved the lives of women not only in the United States but also abroad, as domestic violence is now openly discussed in many countries beyond our own borders. That's the type of community-wide change we aspired to at PT&Co., and in this case we really made a difference.

♪

In addition to my PR work and caregiving to my husband, not to mention dancing, I also volunteer in community organizations. I have sat on the boards of many nonprofits over the years, including the Girl Scout Council of Greater New York; U.S. Fund for UNICEF; the American Friends of the Phelophepa Train, an organization that supports a train that travels throughout South Africa delivering primary health care services to underserved villagers; and Family Violence Prevention Fund, with which PT&Co. had partnered on the Liz Claiborne "Love Is Not Abuse" campaign.

Though my volunteer work added more hours to my

already overtaxed days, I had decided from a young age that I didn't want to have children and that the time I would have spent raising a family I would instead devote to organizations that helped women and children. The Girl Scouts, in particular, have always been dear to me. I tell people I have "green blood," which is Girl Scout speak for someone who is a Girl Scout through and through. My ongoing involvement with the organization began with my membership in Troop 45 when I was growing up in Kaneohe, about twenty minutes from Honolulu. Since 1996 I have sat on the board of the Girl Scout Council of Greater New York, which serves girls ages five to seventeen in the city's five boroughs.

As a board member I usually work with girls in New York City, but in February 2003 I was invited to be the keynote speaker at a gathering of three hundred Girl Scouts from throughout Hawaii at the Sheraton Waikiki on Oahu, my home island.

I boarded the plane, excited to be returning home and eager to be speaking to such a large gathering of Girl Scouts. I knew that many of these bright, young, impressionable girls probably had never left the Islands and, because of that, their dreams of the future might be limited to Hawaii. My goal was to share the story of a Girl Scout from Troop 45 in Kaneohe who dreamed of living in the Big Apple and how she made that dream come true. I wanted to encourage these Girl Scouts to dream big and to tell them that however big their dream, they could accomplish it. And, most importantly, I wanted to let them know that any *new reality* they want to create starts *first* with a dream and a vision.

⌒

My goal was to share the story of a Girl Scout from Troop 45 in Kaneohe who dreamed of living in the Big Apple and how she made that dream come true. I wanted to encourage these Girl Scouts to dream big and to tell them that however big their dream, they could accomplish it.

⌒

It is five thousand miles from New York to Hawaii, and the nearly ten-hour flight always leaves me more than enough time to work, sleep, read, and inevitably drift into memories of living on the Islands. Growing up, I've always felt as if I had been born in the wrong place and time. School, baby-sitting, playing clarinet, and even the Girl Scouts, which I did enjoy, paled in comparison to my movie-fueled fantasies about the high life in New York City. But it wasn't only the lack of nightclubs and Broadway musicals that annoyed me about my birthplace. It was the small-town claustrophobia. No matter which island you lived on, it was too close a community. Everyone knew everyone's business, and the confines of the island necessitated everyone getting along, or at least pretending to.

My late mother, June Tanaka, was a warm, loving person who hugged everyone on first meeting. As a child, going anywhere with her was an incredibly time-consuming proposition because she knew and was liked by so many people and, it seemed, had to stop and chat with each and every one of them. We could be shopping in a town on the other side of the island and she would invariably run into someone she knew. My brother and I always groaned, knowing it would take us twice as long to get anything done because of Mom's friendly nature and the Aloha spirit extended by most residents.

When I was little, my mother was always hugging and kissing us and telling us how much she loved us. All the kids in the neighborhood gravitated to our house because she was everyone's favorite mom. The other kids even called her "Mom," which I found very upsetting because, after all, she was *my* mom and I didn't want to share her love with them. My mother explained to us that love was not a finite thing—you didn't have to worry that if you gave some away, you would have less. In fact, she said, just the opposite was true. The more love you gave away, the more you had to give. For a four-year-old, that was not an easy concept to embrace. Her wisdom about love, along with her oft-repeated advice to "share your toys and cookies," ended up being the rocks upon which I built my life, my agency—everything. But while I was growing up, I sometimes felt Mom's popularity made the Islands a small town, one so small it was going to smother me.

⌣

My mother explained to us that love was not a finite thing—you didn't have to worry that if you gave some away, you would have less. In fact, she said, just the opposite was true. The more love you gave away, the more you had to give.

⌣

As I noted earlier, my view of community has evolved since I first arrived in New York, so eager to escape the nosy neighbors and provincial thinking of "locals" in Hawaii. But reflecting on all this, by the time I landed at Honolulu International Airport, I knew how fortunate I was to have been born and raised in the Islands, where neighbors look after one another and the value of community is woven into the fabric of daily life.

The Girl Scout conference at which I was speaking was called "Teaming Up for Tomorrow," and girls from all over the Islands had been selected to attend. I had given many speeches about PT&Co., but I wanted my Girl Scout speech to be a little different, more inspirational. Looking out at the hundreds of Girl Scouts in khaki uniforms filling the ballroom of the Sheraton Waikiki Hotel, I was struck by how fresh and expectant they seemed, just as I had been at their age. I was slated to talk about my career path from Girl Scout in Hawaii to CEO in New York, but I wanted to tell them about some of the more personal aspects of that journey, things I wouldn't necessarily tell a group of businesspeople. So I spoke about my childhood in Oahu and my fantasies about getting out.

"I believe visualizing your dream helps to make it come true. That which you focus on—good or bad—is what you'll manifest."

"My life in New York is a dream come true, and that's no accident," I said. "I visualized living in New York so often and for so long that I actually manifested living there. Yes, 'manifested' it. I believe visualizing your dream helps to make it come true. That which you focus on—good or bad—is what you'll manifest. That's why I'm not a big believer in spending too much time thinking about worst-case scenarios. I'm afraid I'll manifest exactly what I don't want to happen! Instead, I set a goal and a deadline. And I tell other people about it. Lots of times, the people who love and support you will try to help you reach your goal." I went on to describe how this seemingly simple practice had led to many of my professional successes.

It was the most personal and revealing speech I had ever given up to that point. I even talked about my new goal to bring joy into my life every day. "I've always loved to dance, and in my heart of hearts, if I could be anything, I'd be a dancer. So last year I began studying dance for the first time in my life. It has since become a burning passion for me. I take lessons three times a week, and my new goal is to dance in a competition and someday win a championship."

The place erupted! The Girl Scouts clapped and cheered wildly, and suddenly I was flooded with the support I had been telling them about just moments before. I had stated a goal out loud, and now I had to make it happen. In a sense, every ballroom victory I have earned since that night can be traced to the big Aloha I received from the Girl Scouts at the Sheraton Waikiki Hotel.

INTERMEZZO

The Samba

THE AMERICAN RHYTHM samba, which Tony so skillfully choreographed for my samba showcase, captivated me in the musical *Flying Down to Rio* long before I knew the name of the dance. The ballroom samba evolved from the wilder Brazilian version that can still be seen today, when thousands of dancers—some nearly naked, others in elaborate costumes—frolic their way through the streets of Rio during Carnival. Ballroom samba attempts to keep the spirit of the original while translating it into patterns the average social dancer can learn and enjoy.

If the American Rhythm version of samba were a character from literature, it would be the irrepressible Tigger: bouncy, bouncy, bouncy, and fun, fun, fun! The timing and coordination of the flexing and straightening of the knees gives the dance its characteristic bouncy motion, which looks and feels very different from all the other rhythm dances. Yet the infectious bounce must be quarantined to the lower half of the body. No bobbing heads or rocking shoulders. Stillness but not rigidity upstairs: picture a fluidly moving showgirl balancing a spectacular feathered headdress, and remember that a wobble up top will bring everything crashing. Downstairs is where you throw the party. In the early stages of learning samba, you may feel that your knees and feet should be thrown in the slammer for disorderly conduct, for going a little too crazy and always being in the wrong place at the wrong time. In more advanced stages of learning, the party really takes off, as your feet and knees cooperate and you also roll the hips and flick the pelvis back and forth. (No side-to-side motion allowed!)

The rhythm of samba follows a "one-a-two" syncopated count. Beginners can find it difficult to process that each step taken does not correspond to a single beat of music. The first step, "one" of the count, occurs over three-fourths of a single beat of music. The second step, "a" of the count, takes one-fourth of a beat of music. One beat of music, two steps. The third step, "two" of the count, requires a full beat of music. One beat of music, one step. None of the steps takes the same length of time. Samba is a very lively dance, so it's important to master the rhythm before trying to learn a lot of patterns.

While all the other rhythm dances cover a limited patch of the floor, the samba travels. The Latin or pop music is playing fast, and the dancers smile and bounce as they make their way around the entire floor. With all the hip-rolling and pelvic-ticking, samba is also unabashedly sexy and looks most natural when the dancer feels earthy and vibrant and does not hesitate to show it. Yet perhaps because of the foot speed, rapid coordination, and upper-body stillness required—all of which demand a lot of physical control—samba does not look raunchy or vulgar, it simply exudes the joy of being alive. Alma Guillermoprieto, a former pro-dancer and current journalist, sums up the samba this way: "There is no point to samba if it doesn't make you smile."

CHAPTER 5

The Ballroom World and the Real World

"To dance is to be out of yourself. Larger,
more beautiful, more powerful."

—Agnes De Mille

he New York Dance Festival, where Tony and I would enter our first competition, was a small, local event. We would be competing in six dances: the cha cha, rumba, swing, merengue, mambo, and samba. I didn't like to think about being scrutinized and compared to other couples, but I did need to know the basic rules of ballroom dance competitions. The system used to judge the dancers was bewildering, so Tony explained a simplified version of it to me.

A competition usually took place over three to four days, sometimes fewer and sometimes up to a week for the really big competitions like the Ohio Star Ball. Amateur and Pro-Am events were typically scheduled during the matinee session, which could begin as early as 8 a.m. The evening sessions often featured championships in three categories: *Pro-Am*, where a professional danced with an amateur student; *Amateur*, a couple composed of two amateur dancers; and *Professional*, where two professionals danced, which were the highlight of every competition.

Tony and I would be competing in Pro-Am American Rhythm, a category featuring Latin American music and dances. There were three levels of Pro-Am competition: Bronze (which included Newcomer—our category), Silver, and Gold. Each level was progressively more difficult and had a specific syllabus of approved figures, or series of steps

that comprised a dance routine. You were not allowed to perform figures beyond the syllabus for your level during competitions. If you did, you could be penalized by the judges, who might drop you a placement—for instance, from second place to third.

Dances were performed in rounds called heats, each of which lasted about a minute and a half. Depending on how many other couples were competing, and how well we did, the judges could call Tony and me back multiple times. We might start with a quarterfinal heat that had as many as twenty-four couples, then move to a semifinal heat that had twelve couples, and finish with a final heat involving the top six couples. Only the top three couples in the final heat would receive a placement of first, second, or third. Those who placed fourth, fifth, or sixth were simply designated "finalists."

In preparation for the event, Tony and I practiced our routines for the next two months. Meanwhile, PT&Co. continued to struggle through the recession. In December 2002 the year-end fee income numbers showed a 15 percent decline from 2001. The first few months of 2003 continued the trend—a slow seeping away of business. We won some accounts and we lost some, but the general direction was down. My three dance lessons a week gave me infusions of energy and optimism I badly needed at work and at home.

The year had also not started off well for Assad. In January, he suffered a series of seizures. I counted six in a two-week period. It had been seventeen years since his condition had first been diagnosed, and since then, surgeries, followed by

traditional and alternative cancer treatments, had kept Assad alive and functioning fairly well. These new seizures were more alarming—Assad began drooling out of the left side of his mouth, his left hand went numb, and he had difficulty speaking. A CT scan showed that his tumor had regenerated. His doctor suggested that Assad have the tumor surgically removed yet again, but told us we could wait until the summer.

This would be Assad's third surgery to remove his brain tumor. The first two, in 1986 and 1990, had been successful. He had suffered few side effects, so I fully expected this third surgery to be fairly uneventful and effective, too. I wasn't overly worried. At Assad's urging, I focused my attention on my debut as a competitive dancer. I knew (because close friends told me) that part of the reason Assad was so supportive of my dancing was that he felt terribly guilty for all the caretaking I had to do. The fact that I had this new passion in my life was a big relief to him, and he loved that it made me so happy.

As the festival approached, Tony reminded me that for this event I would need a real costume. "I know just the person to design it," he said. "Lena Kosovich." Nick and Lena Kosovich were a champion dance team who later appeared in multiple seasons of *Dancing with the Stars* and designed many of the costumes on that show. (Nick was also the inspiration for a MySpace fan page called "Sisters of the Protective Order of Nick's Manly Chest." His devotees were legion.) Nick and Lena were retired from professional dancing, and like many former champions, they had branched out to relate

ballroom businesses. The two of them judged competitions and designed and marketed their ballroom dancewear line, LeNique. Because they were dancers themselves, they had a special awareness of what would "show" well on the ballroom floor, knowing, for example, what colors would pop and what styles would flatter every figure.

I arranged to meet Lena at the Manhattan Amateur Competition, a ballroom event for amateur couples that was staged at Barnard College in New York City. Lena had set up a LeNique vendor's booth there. At the time, I had no idea who she was. I was startled to see a statuesque Russian beauty with dark hair, ice-blue eyes, high cheekbones, and a slightly broad Slavic nose. She looked like a raven-haired Uma Thurman, with better posture. Lena quickly sketched out a dress for me and we talked about colors. To be honest, I didn't much like the color she and I eventually chose—a deep ruby pink.

A few weeks later I drove to the LeNique studio in Nyack, New York, for a fitting. Nyack is an arty community along the Hudson River, in a beautiful rural area north of the city. The studio reminded me of an elves' workshop. Bolts of fabric in neon colors lined the walls, shelves were jammed with vats of sparkling rhinestones, and dazzling costumes hung on racks. My dress was made of stretch satin with sheer net sleeves, a boat neck, and a skirt that flared out from my hips to a series of deep scallops just below the knee. A V-shaped inset of the netting wrapped asymmetrically down one side of the bodice, slenderizing the overall look. It was a lovely beginner's dress, not too over-the-top or revealing. I knew that seasoned dancers earn the right to wear heavily "stoned" gowns with plunging backs and necklines, major jewelry, and elaborate hairdos, but beginners like me were expected to be more restrained. That was fine with me. In fact, I didn't want any rhinestones at all on my dress. I thought they were tacky. But Lena assured me that while she would use them, she would do so sparingly, as was appropriate for a beginner. She wouldn't take no for an answer, insisting that I must have some sparkle when I was on the competition floor.

Although I still wasn't crazy about the color of the dress, it felt amazing on me. When I spun, the skirt spun a bit further, making the move more graceful and complete. It felt cos-tumey and girly, and was a far cry from my civilian uniform of dark pantsuits and chunky sterling silver jewelry. I wasn't quite Ginger Rogers yet, but I was heading in that direction.

When the day of the competition finally arrived, I awoke at 6 a.m. to prepare at my apartment. Assad was still asleep; he would arrive at the event later with nearly the same group of friends who had attended the samba showcase. I tiptoed into the bathroom and switched on the light, suddenly not knowing the specific steps to prepare myself for my first dance competition. My hair was still in its short, wash-and-wear style, and there wasn't much I could do with it. Sighing, I slicked it back, away from my eyes, so at least I'd be able to see the dance floor. I wasn't about to wear my glasses. I hadn't yet gotten contacts, but my close-range vision was good enough to get me through the event, as it had in the showcase. I applied what I thought was a lot of makeup (a large amount was required due to the stage lights), slipped into my semisparkly, ruby-pink rhythm costume, which is shorter than a ballroom gown to better show off your legs and knees when dancing, and went downstairs to hail a cab.

Competitors don't wear their ballroom costume, and makeup outside on the street in broad daylight. There's the "real world" and the "ballroom world," and the ballroom world exists inside.

Tony, who was waiting for me in the lobby of the Roosevelt Hotel, a once-grand, midtown Manhattan hotel, burst out laughing when he saw me striding though the front doors. "You just walked down the street like that?" he asked.

"Why not?"

"Nothing. You look wonderful."

I later learned that competitors get dressed at the hotel or competition venue and have their hair and makeup done there as well. They don't wear their ballroom costume and makeup outside on the street in broad daylight. There's the "real world" and the "ballroom world," and the ballroom world exists inside.

I had barely taken Tony's arm when another of his students, Caroline "Kebbie" Kennedy, ran up to me. In her civilian life, Kebbie was the editor of a trade magazine. "Patrice, you look great!" she exclaimed. "But you're not wearing enough makeup." She pulled me into the ladies' room and hauled out a tackle box full of stage makeup. "Stand still," she ordered, and started applying colors with all the subtlety of a first-grader with finger paint.

"That's too much!" I protested.

"No. Just when you think it's enough, you have to put on five times more." She pulled out a pair of false eyelashes.

"Not false lashes! I won't be able to see!"

"Okay, okay. There. You're beautiful." My face looked garish, but Kebbie was right—on the dance floor, under the lights and in motion, it looked fine. This was all part of the theatrical presentation. As you whirled around in front of the judges and audience, it was important that they could tell you had eyes and a mouth! Without the exaggeration of makeup, it was all a blur. The judges noticed every aspect of your appearance. They even expected Pro-Am dancers to take the competition seriously by wearing eye-catching costumes, full makeup, and professionally done hair. I had at least two out of three.

The Roosevelt was an older hotel, grand in its day but a little down on its heels. However, it did have a glamorous, two-story ballroom featuring a mezzanine with an ornate, wrought iron railing. My cheering section was leaning against the railing, watching the action from above. Tony and I were waiting for our event in the lobby outside the ballroom, and as we entered the room, I looked up and waved at Assad and my friends.

That was the last time I noticed them, because the ballroom itself was instant sensory overload. Everyone was in full dress and makeup, and there were people dancing, swirling past one another like at the studio, only the flamboyant costumes and bright stage lights made it feel like the set of an MGM musical. My beginner's costume was very different from the barely there, brilliantly stoned theatrical costumes of the more seasoned competitors surging on and off the ballroom floor. Judges were standing around the floor's perimeter, and an announcer was calling out orders I didn't understand: "Heat 246. Newcomer Bronze. Ladies A in Ballroom A. Ladies B in Ballroom B. Waltz music, please." The floor was divided into Ballrooms A and B, and I didn't know which was which.

I was shocked to see that there was more than one couple on the floor at a time. I had not given much thought to the details of the competition; I had assumed it would be like the showcase, with each couple getting a minute or two to themselves on the dance floor. When Tony and I were standing in the on-deck area (the roped-off, red-carpeted area leading to the ballroom floor), I learned, to my huge relief, that he and I wouldn't be out there all by ourselves. Just before we moved onto the floor for our first routine, a cha cha, I told him matter-of-factly that I hoped I would remember it. He stopped for a split second and looked at me as if to say, "You're kidding, right?" But there was no turning back now. Out we went.

I was in my own world—totally in the moment, not ner-vous, and excited to be dancing. I didn't think about place-ments, nor was I worried about doing well. Between heats I stood shivering at the edge of the floor (ballrooms are always kept chilly) until the announcer would call our heat number and Tony would escort me out for another dance. There was so much going on between the music, the judges, the cou-ples coming on and off the floor, and Tony and I listening for our heat to be called, that I just followed him and tried to dance the routines exactly as we had practiced them. We danced our six Newcomer dances only once each because it was a small competition and each heat was a final round. Before I knew it, we were done.

I was in my own world—totally in the moment, not nervous, and excited to be dancing. I didn't think about placements, nor was I worried about doing well.

Afterward, Assad and the others rushed downstairs, and my husband threw his arms around me.

"You were great," Mr. Sweetheart said as he gave me a big hug. He high-fived Tony and congratulated him on "working me hard," as he had directed him to do some months earlier. "She'll work her heart out to become a good dancer," my husband had told him, and he was right.

We all chatted excitedly while Tony went to see how the judges had rated us. He came back smiling. We had placed first, second, or third in all six dances. "One of the judges really liked your merengue," Tony said. "She was tapping her foot while watching you dance."

She liked my merengue! Pure joy.

Looking back, I remember the thrill of competing, as well as my desire to sign up for another competition right away. I recall the happiness on Assad's face, and how we both avidly watched the competition video later that evening, amazed that I had participated in such a thing. In the video I saw Tony looking up and pointing at Assad, who was standing on the mezzanine. Tony seemed to be saying, "Don't worry, I'm working her hard." Assad felt included in my success and he was happy for me. We went out to dinner that evening to celebrate, and he told me how proud of me he was, and how glad that I had finally found something other than work that I loved to do.

Assad encouraged me to compete in the American Star Ball, which would take place in New Jersey that May. I did. That time, he was the only fan in my personal cheering section, but he was a very supportive and engaged fan, cheering loudly for Tony and me. We won three first places and two second places at that event, and if I wasn't hooked before,

I was now. As we prepared to take Assad in for surgery the following month, my mind was already racing ahead to my next competition, Manhattan DanceSport, which would take place in July.

♪

On June 17, 2003, Assad entered what was then Columbia-Presbyterian to have the surgery for his brain tumor. He developed complications and remained in a semicomatose state for six weeks. Coincidentally, Ellen LaNicca's father-in-law was in the same hospital, and Ellen and her husband, Carl, visited Assad several times. I was there every day, telling him about the plans I had for when he returned home, even though he was unresponsive and I wasn't sure how much, if anything, he understood. Back at the office, I shared a few of my ideas with Ellen.

"If he needs a lot of care, I'll find a nursing home for him near our apartment," I said.

Ellen was quiet for a moment and then she said, "I don't mean to pry, but how are you going to pay for it? They're really expensive."

I had no idea how much nursing homes cost, but Ellen did. The number was astonishing. It would wipe out our savings in less than a year.

Ellen continued, "Unfortunately, Medicare won't cover the cost until you've depleted all of your assets—your home, your car, whatever you have."

I was too shocked to speak. In all the years of Assad's illness, we had concentrated on cures and treatments, most of which were covered by insurance. Long-term care had never crossed my mind. Always practical, Ellen said, "This may sound terrible, but if Assad needs to be moved to a nursing home, you should consider getting divorced. That way they couldn't touch your assets, and he would be cared for."

I sat at my desk for more than an hour, staring out at the dusty summer afternoon and trying to comprehend my options. I couldn't divorce Assad, my husband, Mr. Sweetheart. I remember thinking, *This is just not right.*

My friend Tricia, who used to be a nurse, flew in to help me with Assad for two weeks. I wanted someone to be with him at the hospital when I wasn't there. Tricia, whom Assad had always considered a good buddy, sat and talked to him, even though he was never fully conscious and couldn't communicate. She later told me that she said to him, "If you have to go, don't worry—just go." She wanted to let him know that he didn't have to keep on living just to be here for me. She told him I would be fine. Tricia stayed for two weeks, and when she left, my parents came to help me. My dad and mom were great, staying at the hospital with Assad every day. My mom sat next to him, holding his hand and talking to him. My dad, who is a civil engineer, kept a record of the times and visits of the doctors and nurses each day and documented the readings of Assad's vital signs. Dad left after ten days, but Mom stayed behind, despite Dad's objections. It's one of the only times I can remember her not deferring to my father's wishes. My dad wasn't used to being separated from Mom; he was totally dependent on her. I was so grateful that she chose to stay with me. The night before she was to return home to Hawaii, my mother whispered to Assad that she had to go but would be back soon.

Early the next morning the hospital called to inform me that Assad had died at 5:31 a.m. I couldn't believe it. When we had left that night, he had been more alert than at any time since the surgery. He had even been flirting with the nurses, which to me was a good sign, indicating that he was feeling like his old self.

"Are you sure?" I kept asking the nurse. I just couldn't process the information, but my mother didn't seem surprised.

"He looked at me with such sad eyes when I said I was going home," she told me. "I think he chose to leave now so that I would still be here to help you." I think she was right.

The day Assad died was July 25, 2003. I held a service for him the following week at the United Nations Chapel. We had been married by the UN chaplain in 1987, and I thought it was a fitting venue for our earthly separation. I decided to have a combination service and celebration of Assad's life, with an exhibit of his paintings, which I displayed throughout the chapel. I sent email notices only to close friends whom I thought might want to attend. In my email, I told everyone that I planned to wear hot pink, and encouraged them to dress for a celebration of Assad's life because that's what I intended the service to be.

That morning, I was surprised to find nearly three hundred people filling the pews of the UN chapel. People who came told me it was an inspiring and uplifting service. I spoke about Assad and why he was not only a hero to me, but Mr. Sweetheart as well. I told them about how he and his friends were conscripted by the Russian army, and how Assad eventually made his way to India and later to the United States. I shared with them how Assad's arrival in New York was an accident; his only friend lived in California and that's where he had planned to disembark the plane that had taken him from New Delhi to Hong Kong to Los Angeles (where the group of refugees Assad was traveling with got off the plane for an overnight stay), and finally to New York. Speaking very little English then, Assad didn't understand that Los Angeles was a city in California, so after spending the night in LA, he reboarded the plane. He was left with no choice except to get off in New York and make his home there.

I also told the audience how we met, and about the obstacles to our unlikely marriage. I talked about how glad I was that Assad had decided to be an artist and not a civil engineer, because now I was surrounded by his art every day, and it was a source of great comfort and pleasure to me. I spoke about Assad's courage, grace, and good humor in his seventeen-year battle to survive a brain tumor, and about the countless surgeries and treatments he endured. I told the congregation that Assad never, ever complained about his condition and that, in fact, he considered himself the luckiest man in the world. I said, "For these and many other reasons, Assad will always be my hero and my Mr. Sweetheart."

After the service, I arranged for my close friends and family, who had flown in from Hawaii and Oregon, to gather for dinner at an Afghani restaurant to continue the celebration of his all-too-brief life. I know Assad was pleased.

♪

I truly believe that ballroom dancing taught me how to live again after I lost Assad. His death was a crushing and unexpected blow, although friends later told me they saw it coming. I didn't. Assad and I had already been through so much together that losing him now didn't make sense to me. I felt as if I had been run over by a truck—flattened. All I wanted was to escape, maybe go back to Hawaii for six months to grieve and reflect on what to do next. But that was out of the question because I still had an agency to run. Billings were falling and we were now down 17 percent below 2002. In July 2003, twenty months after the recession officially ended, New York was experiencing a jobless recovery and payrolls continued to shrink.

I kept dancing. My lessons gave me energy and forced me to focus on the present moment for a few blessed hours each week. Now that I was a competitive dancer, I started going to more ballroom events—sometimes to participate, sometimes just to lose myself in the alternate universe of the ballroom world. In the real world, I comported myself as a responsible adult, working hard to meet my obligations. I trudged to work every day, not daring to speak too often about my grief, for fear that if I did, I wouldn't be able to function at all. In the ballroom world, my only obligations were to look glamorous and dance. In my sparkling gowns and elaborate hair and makeup, I left "real world" Patrice Tanaka behind.

In the ballroom world, my only obligations were to look glamorous and dance. In my sparkling gowns and elaborate hair and makeup, I left "real world" Patrice Tanaka behind.

The ballroom world was only a few hours away anytime I liked. Nearly every weekend, a ballroom dancing competition is held in a hotel or resort somewhere in America. Like a nomadic Renaissance village, the ballroom world materialized in Hyatts and Hiltons across the land. This world has its royalty—the promoters and champion dancers. It has its nobility—the top-ranked amateur and professional competitors. It has artisans who set up booths in the hotel corridors and meeting rooms to sell extravagant costumes, jewelry, shoes, and other dance accessories. It has makeup artists and hair stylists to tend to the needs of dancers. It has videographers and photographers to document the event. Finally, it has an audience, many of whom were amateur or professional dancers themselves. Most of these people stay within the hotel complex for the duration of a three- or four-day event, not wanting to break the spell.

In the ballroom world, beautiful dancing and music continue

nonstop every day, from early morning until past midnight, when the final awards are presented to the champions. Competitors are dressed to the nines with flawless, albeit exaggerated, makeup, hair, costume, and jewelry—an impeccable presentation! Like the stars in the Hollywood films I had adored, the denizens of the ballroom world are comfortable flaunting their costumes off the dance floor and in the hotel lobby, dining rooms, and public spaces, creating a fantasy escape from the too-casual real world of T-shirts, jeans, and unkempt hair.

Dancers of all skill levels mingle together, from novices like me to world champions. The professional dancers are an international group, including many eastern Europeans and Russians who had immigrated to the United States to seek their fortunes. Others hailed from South America and places like Haiti and the Dominican Republic, where they had grown up dancing to Latin music. They naturally excel in the Latin and rhythm categories and often compete in smooth and standard competitions, too. The first time I stepped into an elevator with a professional dancer in full costume—a delicate young Russian in a sparkling midnight-blue gown, her skin dusted with glitter—it was like being backstage with a member of the Bolshoi Ballet. You never see creatures like that in "real" life.

Lights, action, music, and drama—all enacted by beautifully groomed and costumed ladies and gentlemen! This is the world of ballroom dance competitions. The judges, too, are impeccably and often theatrically attired in long capes and gowns, standing tall and aloof around the perimeter of the dance floor, every inch the former dance champions that many of them had been. On the elevated stage sit other ballroom adjudicators who monitor the routines performed by the amateur competitors during each heat to make sure they aren't dancing outside the syllabus (unless it is an "open" round, which allowed creative choreography). Presiding at the podium as master of ceremonies is usually John DePalma, whom I think of as the "voice of ballroom." John announces every heat in a strong, unwavering voice familiar to those who compete regularly, intoning, "Heat 239, Open Bronze, Ladies B. Cha cha music, please."

Couples waiting to compete stand nervously in the on-deck area at one corner of the dance floor near the dais. When their heat is called, competitors are allowed to step onto the dance floor and pick a spot where they can be seen and, hopefully, marked for a callback by the judges, or given a placement if they are dancing in a final round. The goal for competitors is to make every callback until the final round and then to place first, second, or third in the finals.

The Pro-Am competition heats begin at 8 or 9 a.m. and continue until about 5 p.m. Then there is an hour or two break to clean and reset the ballroom for the exciting evening championships, when the professionals dance. In my first year of competitive dancing, Tony and I would usually compete at the Bronze level, so my heats were the first ones called. Starting in the early morning meant that my hair and makeup appointments with the stylists who traveled to each competition had to be scheduled for 5 or 6 a.m., or even earlier, depending on how many clients were booked ahead of me. I once had a hair and makeup appointment at 2 a.m.!

Me dancing smooth with Tony Scheppler. That dress moved and flowed so well that it enhanced the graceful, smooth dance.

After hair and makeup it would be time to put on my dance costume, including shoes and eye-catching jewelry to adorn my hair, ears, neck, wrists, arms, and sometimes ankles—all to attract the attention of the judges. The last thing a dancer wants is to find out that the judges didn't see her on the competition floor because their attention was drawn to her competitors. By the summer of 2003 I had started to look and feel a little more feminine—I had lost ten pounds from all the dancing, and I had let my hair grow to shoulder length. I felt comfortable—sexy even—in my costume, makeup, and heels. I was becoming less and less like a student and more and more like the elegant dancer of my dreams.

I had lost ten pounds from all the dancing, and I had let my hair grow to shoulder length. I felt comfortable— sexy even—in my costume, makeup, and heels. I was becoming less and less like a student and more and more like the elegant dancer of my dreams.

As in the real world, I learned that presentation counted in the ballroom world. It wasn't just the quality of one's dancing.

It was also a dancer's appearance, posture, and manners on and off the competition floor. I didn't know any of this in my early days of competing. After dancing a heat, I would sometimes drag myself off the floor dejectedly, cursing myself for a bad performance. Tony would take my elbow, trying to escort me in a stately manner, while I squirmed away, complaining, "Stop pulling me!" Finally he told me, "It totally undermines your dancing if you stand erect with perfect posture, head held high, while you're dancing, and as soon as the heat is over you shuffle off the floor, slumped forward with your head hanging down. The judges notice everything, from the way you dance, to the way you enter and exit the ballroom floor, to how well dressed and well mannered you are outside the ballroom. You have to behave impeccably the entire time you're at a competition because you never know if a judge is watching you while you're eating breakfast in the dining room or using the hotel gym or riding in the elevator."

That made perfect sense to me, and it was one of the things I came to love about the ballroom world: dressing well and behaving well mattered! When I went to a competition, I tried to comport myself graciously. I dressed up for every meal, from breakfast to late-night supper and drinks. It made packing for competition a thoughtful process. Every outfit I wore—the more theatrical the better—had to be accompanied by the perfect handbag, shoes, accessories, and jewelry. In the ballroom world, wearing rhinestones for breakfast was perfectly normal and expected.

One of my favorite pastimes at competitions was to survey the irresistible jewelry, costumes, practice wear, accessories, and dance paraphernalia sold by vendors who set up a colorful bazaar, usually in a meeting room or large corridor adjoining the ballroom. All manner of jewelry—nothing subtle and everything fairly large and over-the-top—was displayed on long, skirted hotel banquet tables. Hanging from portable racks throughout the room were dazzling stoned costumes in every color and style, some more skimpy and revealing than others. The vendors would travel to the different competitions and meet with dancers to design new ballroom costumes, as Lena Kosovich had with me. Custom-designed costumes could be very expensive, starting at about $1,200 for a short rhythm or Latin dress and $2,500 for a long smooth or standard gown. For that reason, many women bought used costumes. The vendors had racks full of them, which customers sold on consignment. It was a way to recoup some of your original investment after you had worn your dress to a number of competitions and finally tired of it.

Some vendors sold practice clothes, such as skirts and tops, as well as men's costumes—mostly black, fitted trousers and white or black stretch shirts, often with stones added. There were also extravagant dress-up accessories for sale. I once bought a peach-hued fox stole that I've worn only once. I don't know what possessed me to buy it, but when I saw it I just had to have it. At the time, in the beautiful bubble of a ballroom competition, it seemed like a reasonable purchase. The ballroom marketplace always had dance shoes for sale; it wasn't unusual for a dancer to need new shoes in the middle of a competition. There were ballroom music CDs, instructional dance videos, and DVDs of major competitions featuring ballroom champions. A fixture at nearly every major ballroom competition was Albert Parker and his wife, Patricia, of Park West Photography. Al was one of the hardest-working people at the competition, taking photos every day from early morning until late at night. He was in constant motion around the perimeter of the ballroom floor, often edging onto the dance floor in his efforts to get the shot a competitor might want to purchase. After competing, dancers made their way to the Park West Photography tables situated in a corner of the ballroom to carefully pore through the three-ring binders containing contact sheets of photos shot by Al in the preceding hours. There were always more than a few must-have photos where he had captured competitors like me in our most dancerly poses.

In addition to still photos, videographers offered dancers videos of themselves competing. These arrangements were made prior to competing so that one of the four to six videographers situated on an elevated platform facing the ballroom floor could be assigned to tape a specific competitor. The tapes were valuable in that dancers—amateurs and professionals alike—could use them to study their performances. It was also a good way to track your improvement from competition to competition.

In the six months after Assad died, I competed in two competitions and attended two others. With each visit, I got to know more dancers and other ballroom regulars. At one competition Tony introduced me to Sam Sodano, the organizer of ballroom's premiere event, the Ohio Star Ball, which PBS broadcast for many years as "America's Ballroom

Challenge." Sam and I had been chatting for only a few minutes when I asked him what he considered to be the biggest lesson a person could learn from dancing.

"Ballroom dancing teaches you to love yourself," he replied. It was such a simple and profound statement, and I immediately thought, *He's absolutely right.*

♪

In 2003 Tony started teaching at a new studio called Stepping Out. Like Pierre Dulaine Studio, Stepping Out was home to many champion dancers, and I had the privilege of watching them almost every time I had a lesson. Now that I was dancing competitively, I had a much better grasp of what I was looking at when they practiced their complex routines. As summer faded and PT&Co. continued to search for new clients, I started watching the professional dancers' work habits more closely. The business world is full of sports analogies about teamwork and pushing yourself, but I had never played team sports. Like lots of women, I tended to roll my eyes at all those jockish metaphors. Now I was curious to see if the ballroom athletes had anything to teach me about winning.

One thing I noticed was that even if they could perform a routine perfectly (to my eyes), the pro dancers would keep practicing it over and over. They were always building on their success one detail at a time, day in and day out. The champions never believed they had reached their goal. JT Thomas, who would go on to become National American Smooth Champion with her partner, Tomas Mielnicki, in 2007 and 2009, told me that she tried to improve "just one thing" in every competition, even something as small as perfecting a single hand gesture during one step in her routine. It was a more manageable approach than trying to improve everything all at once.

The dancer's credo of never arriving at the goal and never achieving perfection, but always improving and evolving, struck me as a good approach to take at the agency during this difficult time. The pressure to get new accounts was overwhelming to many of our staff. It consisted of cold-calling, pitching, soft-selling former clients, tapping old friends—very few people enjoy that type of challenge. Most creative types abhor it. It was easier for them to focus on doing great work and hope that someone else would find new business. I proposed the concept of doing "just one thing" every day as a way to overcome that resistance.

Our senior staff had three main areas of focus: keep current clients happy, make sure we were supporting our employees so that we had the best possible workplace environment, and generate new business. Even in the best of times, the natural tendency was to focus on current clients and let employee morale and finding new business slide. When the economy was bad and agency income was down, that tendency could be disastrous.

I instigated the "just one thing" policy to encourage senior staff to proactively address those latter two focus areas. The idea was to do just one thing each day, no matter how small. To generate new business, they could make one call, write one pitch letter, or research one category or one prospect. To support our employees, they could notice which of the junior staff seemed overwhelmed, talk to the person about it, help him or her set priorities or solve just one problem, and maybe take the person out to lunch. This "one thing" approach was manageable—some days you might spend only twenty minutes on your one task and then bury yourself in current accounts again, but over the course of a month all the twenty-minute efforts would add up.

In early fall of 2003, PT&Co. earned the opportunity to pitch Canon USA's PR account, and I was more aware than ever of the ways ballroom dancing was influencing my approach to business. We met with Canon on a Friday and wowed them in our capabilities presentation. We really liked them and felt we could work well with the prospective clients. Just before our meeting with Canon, Fuji—another camera and film manufacturer—called and invited us to pitch their business. We couldn't take on both companies because it would have been a conflict of interest.

To avoid a situation where we would have had to pursue both new business opportunities until we were hired by one of them, I decided to tell Canon about Fuji's interest in our agency. I gave Canon an ultimatum, saying, "We'd love to work with you, but we can't unless you hire us by Monday at noon. If not, we'll have to pursue the Fuji opportunity." Of course, we had no idea if we would get the Fuji account, but I didn't want to devote 150–200 agency hours putting together a proposal for Fuji if Canon wanted to hire us. By positioning this as a "limited time offer" I created a deadline to push Canon. I now had better things to do than work sixty to seventy hours a week—things like dancing! That desire, plus my decision to express what I felt without trying to censor myself for business appropriateness, inspired me to act boldly with Canon. A few minutes after noon on Monday, the Canon prospect called asking if it was too late to hire us. We went on to have a very successful relationship with Canon USA.

~

We had no idea if we would get the Fuji account, but I didn't want to devote 150–200 agency hours putting together a proposal for Fuji if Canon wanted to hire us. By positioning this as a "limited time offer" I created a deadline to push Canon. I now had better things to do than work sixty to seventy hours a week—things like dancing!

~

In addition to Canon, we won a number of other lucrative accounts in 2003. But by September I could see that we were not attracting enough new business to buck the recession and keep the agency profitable. Two years after 9/11, I had to face the facts: PT&Co. needed to downsize in order to survive. It was not going to be enough to cut everyone's salary. I was going to have to lay off employees, and the layoffs would have to include two of the agency's founding shareholders.

We had been avoiding layoffs for a long time, but in retrospect that probably wasn't the right thing to do. It worked when we split from Chiat/Day, but that was a much smaller staff. We had grown quite a bit since then. Businesses have to downsize if their income is downsized. You can't afford to have more staff than your income allows. By not taking the difficult step of laying off staff as soon as our income dropped, or as soon as we knew it was going to drop, I had jeopardized the entire agency. I had to think about what was best for the group as a whole instead of how to save one individual's job. If it hadn't been for the recession, we might have been able to keep riding out the peaks and valleys with across-the-board salary cuts. But twelve years without layoffs was nothing to be ashamed of, and we had to change to survive.

There were now six founding shareholders at PT&Co. (Frank de Falco had left in 2002, worn down by the stress of being part of a group of high-strung co-owners who each had their own ideas of how the agency should be run and often acted on them.) I ran the agency in a consensus-building management style even though I had the proxy to make all decisions with a few exceptions, such as opening a new office or selling the business. For these larger decisions I needed a majority of the shareholders' votes. But I could unilaterally hire or fire anyone, including shareholders. I had never used or even mentioned that power—it's not how I operated the company. Perhaps for that reason, there was a sense of entitlement among the shareholders, all of whom had been there from the first days of PT&Co. There had always been people who felt that because they were owners, they should not have to perform functions they didn't excel at or enjoy—like generating new business.

Everybody at PT&Co., myself included, had strengths and weaknesses. So who should be let go? Given our situation, whoever was going to remain would have to be willing to get their hands dirty, work even longer hours, make new business calls, and network like crazy in order to attract new clients. Fran Kelly had always put strict limits on the hours she was willing to work—her family came first, which I understood and respected. John Frazier was really uncomfortable getting out from behind his computer and networking. He detested it and resisted doing these types of promotional activities. Both Fran and John were incredibly smart and hardworking and talented, but I needed people who were prepared to do whatever it took to survive and prosper. Fran and John were not.

The decision was excruciating, and I talked about it only to one other colleague and two trusted advisors outside the agency. Both advisors strongly counseled me to handle the termination off-site in order to avoid any potentially damaging confrontations within the workplace. They suggested that I have Fran's and John's personal belongings shipped to them rather than allow them reentry into the office, and I agreed. I conducted individual meetings with Fran and John; both advisors were present in each meeting.

I'll never forget the shock on my colleagues' faces when I told them I was letting them go. There was no screaming or over-the-top display of outrage. Just pain and disbelief and the quiet words, "How could you?" It was brutal. And so 2003, which I came to call my *annus horribilis*, finally drew to a close.

INTERMEZZO

Tango

A BLOOD-RED ROSE clenched between sharp white teeth. A proud señorita held tightly in a man's arms but strictly averting her gaze from his face. Cinematic tango clichés? Perhaps, but they accurately symbolize the passionate union of opposites that is at the heart of ballroom tango's character: tenderness and fierceness, love and hate, need and contempt. To dance the tango is to instantly tap into all those feelings. For me, it can be powerful primal therapy.

The tango was born in the slums of Bueños Aires in the late nineteenth century, among lonely gauchos and immigrants at a time when the number of males in the country vastly exceeded the number of females. Fans and historians argue about whether the tango, which can seem to shift from intimate to detached from move to move, can be linked to the brothel business. It's undeniable that, then as now, being a good dancer could make a man stand out and attract female attention, much like a peacock fanning his magnificent plumage to initiate courtship.

With a great deal of cleaning up, the tango transitioned to the middle and upper classes of Argentina. The cry, "Protect our daughters" pretty much guaranteed that the dance would catch on. When its popularity spread to Europe and America just before World War I, the tango evolved even more. As it adapted to an official ballroom syllabus in the 1920s, the tango kept its center of gravity low, with no rise and fall in the footsteps, lending it a stealthy, catlike quality.

The spine remains tall and fluid so that the body is free and flexible in its response to rapid changes of direction. The partners' hold remains close, but in the international style, which developed in Europe, the partners' bodies connect from rib to hip bone, and the woman's frame shapes dramatically leftward away from the man. Changes from closed position to promenade initiate strong head-snapping movements. *Precision* is the watchword of the international tango. The American Smooth version, also with a wide frame, features long, walking strides and rapid swivels, pivots, and checking actions. The man and the woman evince a commanding, powerful presence. They may dance in the open position, joined only with one hand, and completely separated, making turns and explosive movements apart from each other. The American tango follows a notably slower tempo than the International.

International and American styles differ dramatically from the chest-to-chest, cheek-to-cheek, highly improvisational style of the Argentine tango, which has neither set patterns nor a count to follow. Ferocious adherents of the Argentine tango comment regularly on Internet videos of world-class ballroom tango dancers. The gist: "That is *not* the tango—you have ruined our dance!" There's a whiff of irony in this, for the tango is a melting pot dance with influences from Africa, Cuba, and Europe.

For social dancing in the United States, especially for beginners, the American Smooth version of the tango is most accessible. While there is some overlap of patterns in the other three American Smooth dances—for example, "twinkles" are done for changes of direction in the waltz, foxtrot, and Viennese waltz, albeit at varying tempos—the tango has its own set of unique patterns. The primary counts for tango patterns are slow-slow-quick-quick-slow or quick-quick-slow, quick-quick-slow, but there are others as well. The tango also has unique aspects to its hold. When you follow in the tango, the flattened back of your left hand hooks underneath the leader's right tricep rather than resting lightly atop his right bicep. You are locked in! The leader's right hand lies further in and further down the follower's back than in the other smooth dances, which makes the tango hold more intimate even though the frame is wide from elbow to elbow.

For drama queens, the tango offers an unbeatable showstopper that practically demands an audience. The passionate music inspires powerful movement, and all the sudden turns and changes of direction make a long skirt swirl and fly. Smiling politely or benignly is out! To properly dance the tango, you must utterly devastate your partner with your icy-hot charm.

CHAPTER 6

Practice Failing— with or without Chocolate

"The higher up you go, the more mistakes you are allowed. Right at the top, if you make enough of them, it's considered to be your style."

—Fred Astaire

*T*here were two fewer shareholders at PT&Co., and the remaining staff was tiptoeing around the office as if Mom and Dad had just gotten an ugly divorce. I didn't blame them. John Frazier and Fran Kelly had been laid off after more than a decade with the agency. Not only had I terminated them off-site and had the contents of their desks shipped to them, I had also changed the front door codes so that they couldn't reenter the building. In an agency that had always been about workplace culture, this chain of events was alarming. The whole episode was completely out of character for me, and it was the most painful thing I had ever done. I was determined never to do it again and to attract new business if I had to work twenty hours a day to make it happen.

When my phone lit up one afternoon and "Gene Dunkin/ Godiva" flashed on its screen, my spirits lifted. Godiva Chocolatier was one of our oldest and best clients. Then I remembered that Gene was no longer our contact at Godiva. He had moved up the ladder. So why was he calling me now? *Something must be up.*

Eleven years earlier, after I had led the buyback from Chiat/Day and started PT&Co., we had gone about prospecting new business. I called all the ad agencies I knew and arranged to give capabilities presentations at their offices.

Godiva was one of the first referrals our new agency got from those presentations, and we had been thrilled.

Godiva Chocolatier had then been in business more than sixty years, and we knew the product was going through a bit of an identity crisis. Before we went to meet with the Godiva prospect, we did a miniaudit of epicurean and lifestyle editors at important media outlets, such as *Bon Appétit, Food & Wine,* and the *New York Times,* to get a sense of their perception of the brand.

"Godiva's only about pretty packaging now. It's not about quality chocolate," they said, almost to a person. These were the world's key food influencers, experts who decreed whether spending thirty-two dollars on a pound of chocolates was sinfully indulgent or just a sin (and not worth the transgression). We were horrified at their quick dismissal of Godiva, but we were not really surprised. Their opinion was not necessarily based on flavor or quality. In the world of foodies, it was all about what was new, esoteric, handcrafted in small batches—*artisanal*—so that was what they wanted to write about. Not Godiva, which was so mainstream it was even sold in department stores. There was nothing the culinary cognoscenti loved better than to say something like, "Godiva's overpriced. The best chocolate for that kind of money is Scharffen Berger. They separate their beans by country of origin before roasting them!" Godiva was the whipping boy for conspicuous consumption—not new, not superpremium, not worth the cost.

That was the unhappy news we had to report to the Godiva executives at our first meeting. We took a cab to their

Manhattan headquarters, curious to see what was sure to be a sumptuous "temple of the brand"—perhaps rich walnut paneling, plush carpets, velvet sofas, and silver trays piled high with luscious chocolates. The cab deposited us in front of a nondescript building on Lexington Avenue, and we took the elevator up to a bland suite of offices. The walls were a lifeless beige, the furnishings institutional and corporate, circa 1970. If it weren't for the signage, it could have been a copier company. And there weren't any chocolates.

As unattractive as the Godiva offices were, the people could not have been nicer. Gene Dunkin, the vice president of marketing, was a dapper, bow tie-wearing gent in his fifties. After welcoming us (but not proffering chocolates), he let us in on the big PR campaign they wanted to launch.

"Godiva is going to be a sponsor of the U.S. Open Tennis Tournament!" he proclaimed. "We're spending $250,000 and need help to promote our sponsorship."

It was a good thing we *weren't* nibbling chocolates, because at least one of us would have choked. What were they thinking? *Godiva* emblazoned on the wall behind the sweating, grunting tennis pros? How appetizing. And if foodies thought the brand was too mainstream now, jostling for wall space alongside IBM and American Express would seal Godiva's fate. We explained this to them as gently as we could, but they were unconvinced. Gene and some of the other top executives were avid tennis players, and the U.S. Open was a prestigious event. They were probably looking forward to entertaining their most-valued customers at courtside seats.

"Sponsoring the U.S. Open would be just about the worst thing you could do," I finally told them. "You need to burnish the image of the brand, and instead this will be the nail in its coffin as far as the epicurean media are concerned. If you insist on going ahead with this, you should hire another PR agency, because we can't in good conscience help you execute the absolutely wrong strategy."

Gene and his colleagues were stunned. Always a gentleman, he said, "Clearly you feel very strongly about this. So tell us, if we weren't going ahead with the U.S. Open sponsorship, what should we do?"

Thus began a long and fruitful relationship. Our willingness to forego the business because we cared about getting it right persuaded Gene Dunkin to hire us that afternoon.

The first order of the day was to get the food influencers to focus on what was inside Godiva's pretty packaging—the chocolates themselves. We had to reintroduce the media to Godiva, stressing its quality ingredients, taste, and European heritage. Godiva was a long way from artisanal. It was produced in a factory in Reading, Pennsylvania, not far from its parent, the Campbell Soup Company. But we could truthfully say that it was created in the "traditional style of Belgian chocolates." Godiva was slated to introduce tempting new products, such as Café Godiva and Cocoa Godiva hot beverage mixes, so we had good reasons to contact the media and reacquaint them with the brand.

However, simply sending the food influencers boxes of new Godiva products was not going to change their opinion. We needed to "contextualize Godiva in an epicurean experience"; in other words, to present the chocolates in a gourmet setting among cuisine and beverages that were already favored by the foodies. The challenge was to stage an event enticing enough to lure the jaded food media out of their cubicles during their busy workday.

—

We needed to "contextualize Godiva in an epicurean experience"; in other words, to present the chocolates in a gourmet setting among cuisine and beverages that were already favored by the foodies. The challenge was to stage an event enticing enough to lure the jaded food media out of their cubicles during their busy workday.

—

After much thought, we devised a unique event. We would fly the James Beard Foundation's recently crowned "Rising Star Chef of the Year" to New York and have him prepare a special luncheon for food editors, with the new Godiva products revealed as part of the dessert course. We held the event at the private James Beard House, a charming townhouse in Greenwich Village once owned by the legendary cookbook author and TV personality. The luncheon featured Chef Bradley Ogden from the Larkspur Inn in California. Ogden winning the title that year was a lucky break for us, because we could fly him to New York and create a "must-attend" event for food editors who would otherwise have had to fly to California to dine at his highly acclaimed restaurant. The luncheon was standing room only, and the food was amazing. Best of all, Godiva got coverage in all the major epicurean magazines and food sections of the important newspapers.

For two or three years, we did nothing overtly promotional with Godiva for fear of having the epicurean media once again write off the brand as being only about packaging and promotion. Eventually we felt confident enough to engage in consumer promotions, but we had to be very careful not to undo all our hard work. Each year, Godiva introduced different seasonal collections for occasions such as Valentine's Day, Easter, Mother's Day, Father's Day, and Christmas. We decided to support the Valentine's collection because we determined that if we could increase those sales even a few percentage points, it would have a huge impact on revenues for Godiva's entire fiscal year.

Our challenge was to create a promotion that was luxe and classy and a real sales driver yet wouldn't require an investment so big that it canceled out the extra revenue. So we brainstormed. What happens on Valentine's Day? There are engagements. It's a romantic holiday. People give gifts of jewelry, flowers, chocolates, and fragrances—those are the big four. What if we tried to do something in conjunction with one of the other three gifts, knocking one competitor out at the gate? And which of those three would best burnish the Godiva Chocolatier brand? Jewelry—the most premium type of jewelry? Maybe chocolates and diamonds.

The idea we came up with was a very simple sweepstakes. There is nothing more déclassé than a sweepstakes, so we never uttered the "S" word out loud. But that's what it was—an elegant sweepstakes we called "Chocolates & Diamonds." We seeded three boxes of Godiva Valentine's Day chocolates with golden tickets, Willy Wonka style. Each golden ticket would entitle the bearer to a $10,000, flawless, one-carat diamond ring. Hundreds of thousands of boxes of Godiva's "Love in Bloom" Valentine's Day collection were produced, but only three contained the winning golden tickets, for a total prize expenditure of $30,000.

We went out the third week in January with a promotion that was what we in PR call "telegraphic," or easy to communicate in a few words. We called our media contacts and simply said, "Godiva's doing a Valentine's promotion. Buy a box of chocolates and you may win a $10,000 diamond ring that might come in handy this Valentine's." In that first week, our campaign generated five hundred television news segments on stations across the country. Within the three-week window leading up to Valentine's Day, we generated more than seven hundred news stories, representing 150 million media impressions—a tremendous amount of coverage in a concentrated period of time. That first year, Godiva's

Valentine's sales increased 15 percent over the previous Valentine's, attributable solely to our "Chocolates & Diamonds" promotion. There was no advertising; there was no other marketing support aside from point-of-sale material. The "Chocolates & Diamonds" promotion was so successful that it actually increased revenues for the company 7 percent for the entire fiscal year. Gene Dunkin and Godiva were extremely happy.

We continued the "Chocolates & Diamonds" promotion for seven years, changing the diamond prize every year to keep it fresh and newsworthy. One year the grand prize was a ruby, emerald, and diamond necklace that had belonged to the late Jacqueline Kennedy Onassis. It wasn't exactly beautiful, but it had diamonds and, most of all, a newsworthy provenance. We toured the necklace around the United States, displaying it at Godiva boutiques and key department store retailers.

Then, in year seven of the promotion, Gene Dunkin hired a new director of marketing to manage the PR effort. He was a smart, funny guy. We liked him a lot. But he was a guy's guy and didn't understand the promotion. He loved cars, especially BMWs. So instead of "Chocolates & Diamonds," he changed the Valentine's Day promotion to "Chocolates & a BMW." We resisted, explaining that as cool as a BMW was, it wouldn't hit the right note. You might as well say, "Chocolates & a Big-Screen TV." But he was adamant. We tried to add a diamond key ring, just to keep diamonds in there somehow, but at the end of the day it was a car promotion.

It didn't do as well as in previous years. We didn't get a lot of media coverage because the media didn't find "Chocolates & a BMW" as whimsical and romantic a story as "Chocolates & Diamonds." Of course, any promotion loses its luster over time. The media goes on to other things. Soon thereafter, Godiva launched a gorgeous new ad campaign called "Diva." They were moving away from promoting Godiva as a gift-giving product and instead wanted to position the chocolates as an indulgence that women might purchase for themselves.

As part of the "Diva" campaign, I suggested the ultimate female splurge. *Sex and the City* was at the peak of its popularity, so I said, "Let's seed golden tickets for something completely over-the-top. Let's have the grand prize be fifty-two pairs of Manolo Blahnik shoes—one for every week of the year—along with fifty-two boxes of Godiva chocolates. We could also offer fifty-two runner-up prizes of one pair of Manolos and a box of chocolates." The promotion did incredibly well, and we thought we were back in business.

But now Gene was on the phone, regretfully telling me that they had decided to take Godiva and their "Diva" campaign to another PR agency. It wasn't about our creativity or strategic thinking. He said our work had been terrific. But their "Diva" campaign needed real-life divas, and their new PR agency had strong contacts with celebrities. At the time, we did not.

Godiva had been with us for eleven years, a long run for a client-agency relationship. The funny thing was—and we still joke about it—in all those years they never offered us chocolates when we visited their offices. The only time we were treated to Godiva chocolates was when they were launching a new product and wanted us to sample it in clinical, taste-test fashion. Still, our relationship with Godiva had been a fine romance. Now, just when we needed to hold on to every client we could, it was especially hard to say good-bye.

♪

On PT&Co.'s fifth and tenth anniversaries, we had thrown parties for our clients, friends, and families to thank them for their past support and announce our plans for the future. We had staged our fifth-anniversary celebration like a five-year-old's birthday party. Our invitation was a collage that included photos of PT&Co. employees when they were age five. Here's mine:

Me in a pink tutu my mom made me for a friend's costume birthday party. I had never taken ballet lessons, but I was mad about being a ballerina.

Technically, that was the first time I publicly acknowledged my longtime dream of being a dancer. I also brought this one to the party:

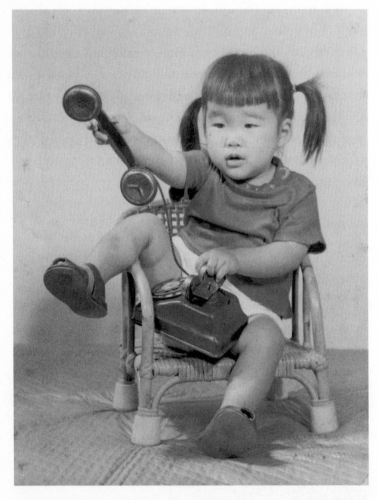

Already working the phones at an early age. If they'd had computers then, I would have been on one of those, too!

Between them, those two photographs had done a good job of forecasting my future.

The fifth-anniversary bash took place at WonderCamp, a children's play space in Manhattan. We served food that a finicky five-year-old would eat, like peanut-butter-and-jelly sandwiches. We also asked the guests to bring gifts for a five-year-old, and we donated the nearly two hundred wrapped presents to local orphanages and hospitals. For PT&Co.'s tenth anniversary, we had a more grown-up affair in a trendy lounge, with passed hors d'oeuvres and cocktails. But now, heading into our fifteenth year, we were stumped. How would we grow the agency? Business was down nearly 10 percent from the previous year, and before I had let John and Fran go we had already reduced shareholder salaries by 10 percent. We wanted to celebrate the fifteen-year mark with expansive new plans, but it wasn't possible. Anything expansive, such as developing another category of industry expertise, or another capability such as branding and marketing, or opening another office in a key geographic market such as Los Angeles, would require an investment. We just didn't have the money.

Slowly it sank in that the only way to expand would be to merge PT&Co. with another agency; in essence, to sell it. Over the fourteen years since starting PT&Co., nine of the thirteen cofounders had either left the agency or the PR profession or had moved from New York, leaving four remaining partners: Ellen, Evelyn, Maria, and me. When I first mentioned this option to the others, they were distraught. Surely there had to be another way to envision a bigger, brighter future. But month after month, we couldn't figure out what that other way might be.

It's not as if I loved the idea myself. The thought of giving up control was scary. Although PT&Co. was operated largely as a collective and the revenues were shared, I maintained the leadership role. That would not be the case if we sold the agency, and the perfectionist in me hated that idea. If I didn't have the final word, I feared we might fail to do great work. Fear of failure had always driven me to overwork myself and micromanage others. Yet by this time, my ideas about failure had been challenged by what I saw every week at the ball-room studio.

—

The thought of giving up control was scary . . . If I didn't have the final word, I feared we might fail to do great work. Fear of failure had always driven me to overwork myself and micromanage others.

—

From my very first lesson, I had been surprised by how many other couples were on the floor at the same time as Tony and me. It was intimidating. They were all better dancers than I was, and some were world champions. The crowded dance floor also annoyed me—*Why did all these people have to get in my way?* But Tony said it was excellent practice for navigating the ballroom floor during a competition.

Not only was the studio dance floor crowded during lessons, it was also ringed by chairs where people sat observing the dancers. When you're a perfectionist, the last thing you want is an audience watching you make mistakes. In this studio, there was no way around it. I had never thought of myself as a performer, and all of a sudden here I was performing badly in front of strangers.

For the first several weeks, I had begun each lesson in a cold sweat of self-consciousness. After a while, I understood that if I repeated a movement or figure enough times, I would eventually get it right. And that is what everyone in the room was doing, including the professional dancers who waltzed and tangoed past me with such grace and skill. Occasionally I would stay at the studio after a lesson and watch International Latin champions Yulia Zagoruychenko and Riccardo Cocchi, or American Rhythm champions Jose DeCamps and Joanna Zacharewicz, practice their routines. They'd laugh if they really blew it, sometimes turning a misstep into a pratfall or a graphic bump and grind. "Failing" to do a step correctly didn't bother them. They didn't perceive it as failure. They were just practicing their steps and routines until they got it exactly the way they wanted it.

—

"Failing" to do a step correctly didn't bother them. They didn't perceive it as failure. They were just practicing their steps and routines until they got it exactly the way they wanted it.

—

Marianne Nicole, a former ballroom champion, highly influential competition organizer, judge, and coach, once told me that the hardest people to teach were doctors because they were so afraid of making a mistake. "If I fail, I'm not a failure," she said. "I just have to approach the routine in a different way. Dancing allows you to experiment with different ways to succeed."

All the top-ranked champions put in at least three to four hours of practice every day. Their bodies were strong and beautiful, without an ounce of fat, and their talent was awe-inspiring, yet they treated me and the other novices like fellow dancers. Before long, my self-consciousness began to fade. The ballroom studio became a laboratory for me, a fun and safe place where I could practice failing in front of other people. My lessons were the one time during the week when I knew I would laugh, forget myself, and just feel good. Soon

I really didn't care who was watching me. It was all part of the process of learning new dance steps and routines.

I had worked in front of people for years—to this day my desk is out in the open, with no walls separating me from my coworkers. But *creating* in front of others, in a domain that was new to me, was different. A lot of the creativity at PT&Co. took place inside our heads while we were at the computer, or standing in the shower, or walking the dog. By the time we got together to brainstorm, I'd have most of the "failure" part of the creative process already worked through. I had four criteria: 1) Would my concept bring to life the strategy we had set with the client? 2) Did it involve a "breakthrough" creative idea? 3) Was it the most efficient way to achieve the client's goals? 4) Was it within the tolerance set of our clients in terms of budget, timing, operational constraints, and cultural fit with their organization? If the answer was yes to all four, I would present my idea to the team.

Dancers, I learned, created their routines in an entirely different way. The process was collaborative, even if one partner was the primary choreographer. The success of the dance depended upon both partners being able to shine. The missteps and corrections had to be worked through together. You couldn't just present your idea fully formed and insist that your partner comply. Well, you could, but from what I witnessed over the years with ballroom professionals, those partnerships didn't last very long. So the top professionals in the strongest partnerships tried, failed, adjusted, and created together on the dance floor.

～

The success of the dance depended upon both partners being able to shine. The missteps and corrections had to be worked through together. You couldn't just present your idea fully formed and insist that your partner comply.

～

The top-ranked champions always evolved from competition to competition. They fine-tuned their routines up until the very last day before an event, and sometimes up until a few hours before. If they could make the routine more dynamic, they were going to go for it, whether or not they could execute the new steps perfectly. They knew that the judges typically worked at competitions every weekend, and what excited them was to see improvement in the routines and in the dancing. Although the level of talent was phenomenal, neither the judges nor the dancers were aiming for "perfection." Perfection didn't exist. It was an unattainable goal. Even Tony, who had been dancing professionally for more than twenty years, continued to take classes with former ballroom champions and was like a kid in a candy store when he learned something new.

In the ballroom studio, I thought about the whole concept of people wanting to be perfect, myself included. If you set perfection as your goal, it creates all kinds of problems that could disenfranchise the people you work with, demoralize them, and prevent you from getting beyond where you think perfection is to a place that might be even better. As my colleague Frank de Falco once said, "Perfection is an overrated virtue."

When I watched the champions practice the same move three, five, or even ten times in a row, I was fascinated to see that when they messed up, they didn't stop and berate themselves. They just tried again. They might get frustrated, but they didn't waste time with self-flagellation. The typical reflex when most of us are first learning a physical activity is to utter a constant stream of self-judgment, like I did: "I'll never get this step. Why do I keep messing up? What's wrong with me today?"

When I did this, I would hear a voice back. It was Tony's. "Stop talking!" he would demand (nicely, but forcefully). "It only gets in the way. Move with me. Just dance."

This was not easy. Quieting that inner critic required as much effort as learning the new steps. It took me a while, but I finally managed. Tony was right: I could master my figures and routines more easily and quickly when I focused completely on learning the steps, rather than dividing my energy between learning the steps and judging myself as I did it.

Once I could see that I was judging myself as I was trying to learn, self-conscious about practicing in public, and nervous about not doing it perfectly the first time—and let go of those things—learning became so much easier. Now, eager to apply every new tool I could to our agency, I decided to try that approach at work.

I started with our brainstorming sessions. I had always tried to go with the flow, but I couldn't help applying my four criteria to everyone else's ideas as well as my own. Now I told myself, "We're just throwing ideas around. It doesn't have to be perfect. It doesn't have to be fully formed." I knew that if I shut other people down just because their concepts didn't meet my four essential criteria, they might think, "Why should I bother to participate?" Then we'd risk losing a germ of an idea or an insight that might not be perfect but could contain a valuable piece of the final concept.

My new approach worked especially well with millenials, the twentysomethings who made up a good part of our junior staff. Because they were young and had so much energy (which is important in the PR business), they sometimes focused on doing things they thought were cool and interesting rather than on an idea that was strategic or the most efficient solution to a problem. I learned to balance my desire to produce results efficiently with an equally strong desire to make sure the millenials (and all my colleagues) were fully engaged and committed to doing the work, even if it meant doing it in a slightly different, sometimes more cumbersome fashion than I might have chosen.

One interesting test of my new approach to "failure" happened in 2007, after I had been dancing for five years. We were pitching the Council for Responsible Nutrition (CRN), a trade association for the dietary supplement industry, which represents manufacturers and ingredient suppliers of vitamins, minerals, herbs, and other botanicals. CRN wanted to hire a PR agency to combat a problem that had dogged the industry since its inception. Every few weeks, it seemed, a study would surface that disproved the safety or efficacy of one supplement or another. Then a leading health reporter or consumer activist would pipe up, questioning the wisdom of taking supplements. Many of the studies were designed to test whether a supplement was a cure for a medical condition or disease, whereas the industry took the position that supplements were not a cure but part of an ongoing regimen of health and wellness. But no matter how the industry protested, the media loved to trumpet the latest debunking story: "A daily multivitamin is a waste of money!" Naturally, that was the kind of thing that drove the supplement industry crazy.

CRN wanted a public relations campaign that would generate positive media coverage for supplements to offset the ongoing drumbeat of negative news stories. Moreover, they wanted to position taking supplements as a mainstream rather than a "fringe" practice. With that in mind, we came up with what we all thought was a clever campaign theme: "What's SUPP?" It used a colloquialism to playfully raise the question about supplements and make them more accessible.

CRN hated it. They said it sounded too much like a popular advertising campaign for a beer brand.

The good news was that they liked our agency well enough to hire us anyway, trusting that we could come up with something better. For the next couple of weeks we brainstormed, and I directed the team not to spend any energy thinking about the rejected first attempt. One benefit of my leadership status was that I could psychologically release my colleagues from the fear of another "failure." After two weeks, we came up with a new theme: "Life . . . supplemented."

This time CRN loved it and gave us approval to move forward. The "Life . . . supplemented" campaign launched with a consumer-education program based on what we called the "Three Pillars of Health": healthy eating, supplements, and exercise. By sandwiching supplements between "healthy eating" and "exercise," we promoted the responsible use of supplements, which was CRN's platform. We also proactively addressed the pushback the industry got from dietitians and nutritionists—namely, that people should get their nutrients from food, not pills. We agreed, but pointed out that in reality, people don't eat healthy foods 100 percent of the time. Hence the need for supplements.

Beyond the skepticism of dietitians and nutritionists was the ongoing "Supplements debunked!" news problem. We found the solution within a rather astonishing figure the CRN executives had tossed out while they were lamenting supplements' supposed fringe status.

"How many people in the United States actually take supplements?" I asked.

"About 150 million," replied Judy Blatman, then vice president of communications at CRN.

"A hundred and fifty million out of a population of

305 million, and you're wringing your hands about being fringe?" We were practically giddy. "Supplements are already mainstream," I told them. "We just need to recognize and celebrate the people who take them, and use those people to persuade the other 155 million Americans to take supplements, too."

We christened the 150 million supplement-takers the "Wellness Cohort" and built a website dedicated to them: www.lifesupplemented.org. Along with tips on healthy eating and exercise, and lots of information about supplements, the website publicized studies we commissioned of doctors and other health care professionals revealing the fact that 72 percent of physicians in America take supplements and 79 percent recommend them to their patients. This implied seal of approval from physicians addressed consumers' confusion about supplements and short-circuited the negative news stories.

"Life . . . supplemented" was a strong, tight campaign, and CRN was happy on many levels. But as far as they were concerned, we had not delivered the ultimate prize: the *Today* show or *Oprah*. Why wouldn't those major outlets help us spread the news that 79 percent of doctors recommend supplements? Because it would seem like they were advising viewers to use them. Given the way supplements were generally portrayed in the media, that was just not going to happen. So Judy Blatman was not at peace. The CRN members wanted the *Today* show, and if we were not delivering the *Today* show, the campaign was a failure.

We had to bring Judy around and enlist her help in

bringing the CRN members around. Our task was to reframe "success" for this client, given the industry, the challenges, and the reality of new versus traditional media. Some CRN members were wedded to traditional media, but for the supplement industry, that wasn't the most effective coverage. "When people have a health concern, they don't turn on the *Today* show, they Google," we reminded them. Our CRN clients were unconvinced that we should focus on online media. They also didn't think we should engage in social media for the campaign. Yet social networks were quickly becoming the best place for conversations about health and wellness, and we had frequent discussions with CRN about that, too.

By the end of the second year of the "Life . . . supplemented" campaign, our CRN clients had modified their definition of success and began slowly to embrace online and social media. We launched a Blogger's Breakfast and Webinar to further communicate the Three Pillars of Health message. We got even more heavily into social media in year three of the campaign with an initiative called "America's Wellness Challenge." By doing so, we were able to exponentially increase the campaign's effectiveness by every metric used to measure its success. What was initially conceived as a three-year campaign by CRN has continued into year four and is on its way to becoming an ongoing industry program.

Creating the "Life . . . supplemented" campaign involved continually fine-tuning the program, oftentimes learning more from our failures than our successes. Thanks to ballroom dancing, I had developed a very different relationship with the "F" word. I viewed failure as a necessary part of a person's, organization's, or campaign's growth. The better you were at learning from your failures, the more success you could generate going forward. The more quickly you learned from your failures, the more quickly you could succeed.

While we had been successful in building PT&Co., by some measures even beyond our wildest dreams, the evolution of our agency to the next level—a bigger, national, midsize PR agency—was possible, ironically, because of our missteps and failures.

While we had been successful in building PT&Co., by some measures even beyond our wildest dreams, the evolution of our agency to the next level—a bigger, national, midsize PR agency—was possible, ironically, because of our missteps and failures. Within eight years, my partners and I had created an employee-owned agency that had been named by *Inside PR* as the "#1 Most Creative" and the "#2 Best

Workplace" among all PR agencies in America. Ketchum, one of the world's largest global PR firms, was ranked #2 and #1, respectively, on those lists. Our emphasis on great work and a humane, supportive workplace had stretched our budget to the point where it was impossible to expand or even maintain our current level of operation, but those same policies had attracted the top talent that made PT&Co. a valuable and coveted entity. If we decided to sell our agency, we would have our choice of corporate suitors, even though we had failed to grow larger on our own. And we would be able to hold on to the talented people who currently worked at PT&Co.

Ballroom dancing taught me how to fail quickly so that I could succeed more quickly. The method many dancers employ is simple: try something and see if it works. If it doesn't, try something else until you find something that does work and that you like. When you want to upgrade your routine to a higher level of difficulty and artistry, experiment through trial and error. That's the only way to grow as an artist or as a business.

INTERMEZZO

Rumba

BE PREPARED TO try, try again when learning to dance the rumba. Many a beginning dancer can't even bear to make eye contact with her partner while in the close, compact, Latin hold of this dance. Only arms and hands are touching, but there's not a lot of air space separating the two partners. It can feel frighteningly intimate. Would you gaze into the eyes of a teacher, coworker, or neighbor? With the rumba, no matter how dramatically you're undulating your hips and ribs, you cannot simply stare past your partner's shoulder with the occasional deer-in-the-headlights blink. You cannot watch your feet as if they might run away if not closely policed. The rumba without eye contact is like Valentine's Day without chocolate.

In their daily lives, adults usually comport themselves with the polite distance of a minuet. At most, they might graze someone's fingertips or brush a shoulder. You will need to shake off this stiffness to let the rumba music in and your emotions out. If a hearty handshake or an air kiss is your idea of connecting with an acquaintance, the rumba will be a jolt to your system. Why risk it? One technical reason: Cuban motion, the rhythmic shifting and settling of the weight of your hips, is the core motion of the rumba, and done at a faster tempo it is the heart of many other rhythm and nightclub dances, from cha cha to salsa. These Latin-infused rhythm dances need not be confined to the ballroom scene or the occasional wedding reception—you can dance them anywhere popular Latin music is playing and there's a scrap of dance floor available.

Another reason you could come to appreciate the rumba is that it is one of few public activities that allows an expression of sexual self-confidence. To really rumba is to announce to the world that you believe in the beauty of your body and its sheer physicality. If you've lost your groove, or perhaps allowed the sands of time to dim its sparkle, the rumba will help you get it back.

Think of Sade crooning "Smooth Operator" or Michael Buble and Nelly Furtado trading the yearning, breathless question "Quando, quando, quando? When will you be mine?" To this hypnotic beat, the rumba begins simply, with a pattern known to anyone ever forced into cotillion by parents: the box step. The couple steps to the side and closes the feet: quick-quick. The leader steps forward and the follower steps back: slow. Step to the other side: quick-quick, and then the follower steps forward and the leader steps back: slow. The Latin feel comes both from the smallness of the steps with turned-out feet and the timing of bending and straightening of the knees, which telegraphs into sway at the hips. In more advanced stages, ribs undulate in the opposite direction from the hips, but shoulders and head always remain level.

You do not cover much ground in the rumba, so if your arms were held wide or if you stood poised over the center of your feet as you would in a dance like the waltz, you would not get a strong sense of momentum of the partner's weight moving. In the Latin hold, you stand slightly forward, weight more toward the front of your feet, feeling a bit of compression, mainly at your gently joined hands, from your bodies pressing toward each other. Not too much. You should match each other in tone, which requires sensitivity, and, in the beginning, trial and error. For the leader, this often means decreasing arm and shoulder strength so as not to over-power the follower. For her part, the follower should neither offer the tone of a wet noodle nor squeeze so tightly or press so hard that she seems about to launch a thumb war or an arm wrestling contest.

In the rumba, the couple's hand-hold looks like a train car coupling, with his hand turned sideways to form a hook and her hand hooked down to fit over it. This allows both compression (leaning slightly into your partner) and leverage (generating outward tension). Leverage allows the couple to keep time and look fantastic when they move apart for things like open breaks and circular walks. Without leverage, your movement can appear loose or out of sync. The concept of compres-sion and leverage is essential to all rhythm and Latin dances. Rumba is a safe haven to master it, because even the rumba steps that are counted as a "quick," covering one beat of music, are relatively slow. Often called the dance of love, the rumba derived from fast and, frankly, erotic dances in the African slave community in Cuba. From that origin it became a sensual ballroom basic for couples who may not even know each other, much less be enamored. Good dance teachers exhibit remarkable patience and kindness with their students when teaching this dance. As professionals highly trained in the use of the body, they feel as little embarrassment observing and working with you as a mid-wife would feel at a birth. In teaching you rumba, your instructor will be sharing a way to release emotional power in a controlled but expressive way. Never graphic or vulgar, but unmistakably seductive, the American Rhythm rumba offers many patterns as intricate and beautifully interac-tive as a new romance.

CHAPTER 7

Partnering for Success in the Ballroom and in the Boardroom

"Those move easiest who have learn'd to dance."

—Alexander Pope

$\mathscr{M}$any agencies had approached me over the years in the hopes of acquiring PT&Co. When we finally decided to do it, I knew of only one agency that was the right fit: Carter Ryley Thomas (CRT). Though it would be several years before we joined forces as one company, I had first met Mark Raper and the other founders of CRT at their headquarters in Richmond, Virginia, in May 2002. Mark had opened that meeting by saying, "At Carter Ryley Thomas, we believe in the abundance mentality." I instantly thought to myself, *I want to play in the same sandbox as these guys.* It turned out that from that very first meeting, Mark had the same goal in mind.

Carter Ryley Thomas was a PR agency much like ours. They, too, had once been a subsidiary of a large advertising agency, where they had felt like the poor stepchild of the all-powerful ad department. The three principals at CRT—Mark, Mike Mulvihill, and Brian Ellis—had reacted just as we had and bought back their agency. They immediately established Carter Ryley Thomas as a family- and employee-friendly company. To underscore their commitment to those values, they named the agency not after themselves but after their children. Carter was one of Mark Raper's daughters, and Ryley and Thomas were the sons of Mike and Brian, respectively. CRT's focus on workplace culture was more than name-deep. Like us, they had been honored as the "Best PR Agency to Work for in America" by the influential PR trade outlet the *Holmes Report*.

When Mark invited PT&Co. down to Richmond, he had also invited three other PR agencies—PainePR (Los Angeles), Padilla Speer Beardsley (Minneapolis), and Peppercom (New York)—which all enjoyed national reputations for creating award-winning work and having a supportive workplace culture. Mark told us all that he wanted to discuss our five agencies working together in some informal way. What we had in common was an understanding that in a professional-service business like public relations, you're only as good as the people who work for you. You have to take care of your coworkers first, so they will be motivated and equipped to take care of your clients. The two are inextricably linked, but at the time, most PR agencies didn't see the connection.

The meeting in Richmond in 2002 resulted in our five agencies founding the Lumin Collaborative, a group whose goal was (and still is) to share intelligence about the forces that affect PR, always focusing on "what's next" that will impact our business and our clients. The five Lumin agencies worked at times to pitch new business together and at other times competed against one another for accounts. It was friendly competition at its best. I loved how these five top-ranked and highly regarded agencies collaborated so well together and operated with a good deal of trust in one another. It was a great example of successful partnering that taught me a lot.

At Lumin meetings we felt free to share strategies (but not proprietary client information), learn from one another, and even admit where we had screwed up so others in the group might avoid making the same mistakes. We also pooled our resources to conduct research, yet we remained distinct entities.

Later it struck me that Mark Raper was conducting another type of research. He wanted Carter Ryley Thomas to be a major, national PR agency, and to do that CRT needed a New York presence. It made sense to acquire a like-minded, well-respected agency that was already established, as opposed to starting a New York CRT office from scratch. In the Lumin Collaborative, Mark had the opportunity to work with all four PR agencies, a kind of courtly dance that would allow him to audition potential partners. He liked what he saw in us, and he approached me about a merger in September 2004.

By the time Mark made the offer, I was more than ready to accept. Even with only four remaining partners, running PT&Co. was exhausting, partly because of the personalities involved. And although I still loved creating breakthrough PR campaigns and forging relationships with clients, I was weary of the uphill battle it had become to grow our business. No matter what we wanted to do—add another capability, open another office, make additional hires—it required investment funds we didn't have. Meanwhile, Carter Ryley Thomas had big plans for our combined agencies.

The New York office would be the beginning of an expansion that would help our combined agencies grow to a larger, midsize firm with $30 million in fees. PT&Co. was currently at $4 million in fee income and Carter Ryley Thomas was at about $6 million. Together we would become a $10 million agency. The business plan was to grow through organic growth and other acquisitions and mergers. For PT&Co. to get from $4 million to $30 million on its own without any investment spending would be impossible. This opportunity was too good to turn down.

Frank de Falco, still one of my closest friends, listened to me mull over the decision many times in the weeks and months following Mark's proposal. Later he told me, "If you hadn't gotten involved with ballroom dancing, you never would have agreed to this. It took all that partnering in dance to prove to yourself that someone else could lead and you could be happy following."

~

"If you hadn't gotten involved with ballroom dancing, you never would have agreed to this. It took all that partnering in dance to prove to yourself that someone else could lead and you could be happy following."

~

Frank knew me well. After all, he was the one who had dubbed me "Ayatollah Tanaka," a nickname that annoyed yet also delighted me because it was so apt. I was incensed beyond all measure by sloppy thinking and sloppy execution. And I was at times autocratic and arrogant in believing that my ideas were the best and if only they prevailed, our client campaigns would win awards and our company would succeed. Naturally I led with my strengths, which meant that anything that was not a strength of mine did not inform the enterprise. My greatest strength had always been to come up with creative and strategic solutions. I could find a solution for anything—sometimes an elaborate solution, if that's what was required. In fact, I had started PT&Co. because I was trying to figure out how to avoid firing the four people who had worked on the Korbel Champagne account when we lost the business. Ultimately my solution was, *I'll form my own agency, and then the decision to fire or not to fire will be mine, not Chiat/Day's.*

My worldview at the time was not so much about running a successful agency as it was about having the best possible team so that we could do exceptional work. I was very good at the client service piece of public relations but not so good at running a profitable business. Some of the biggest mistakes we made at PT&Co. were the direct result of my laser-like focus on doing great work, no matter what it took. With Liz Claiborne, we overworked the account by 450 percent in the first few years. It was our first big-name client, we wanted to succeed wildly—and we did. We won forty awards for the "Love Is Not Abuse" campaign we created for

Liz Claiborne (it was eventually cited by the *Holmes Report* as one of the Top Five PR Campaigns of the Decade), and from that we got a lot of other business. But no agency can over-service accounts like that and run a profitable business. Over time, we reined ourselves in and reduced the overservicing on Liz Claiborne and other accounts, but for a number of years our overservicing levels in the pursuit of doing great work was through the roof.

Meanwhile, what I felt were my strengths influenced the agency in other ways. I relentlessly edited everyone's copy; I stayed at the office past midnight reformatting proposals because I wanted them "my way"; I took center stage at all new business presentations; I urged staff members to mold their creative input to the four-criteria standard I had developed for myself, and in general I micromanaged most of the client-service elements of PT&Co. I sincerely believed this was the only way to ensure that our agency produced outstanding work, but it was the classic behavior of a fearful perfectionist who needed to control every situation in order to make the world a less frightening place.

Years later I asked Ellen LaNicca how the team had felt when I started taking dance lessons and released a little of the control. "To be honest, it was a difficult transition," she said. "Before, we knew that if we were developing a client campaign or a new business pitch, you'd be there from early in the morning until the wee hours of the night. You were totally involved. We went from that to watching you leave the office to go dancing. At first we wondered if you had lost the commitment to build the agency. It took about a year to adjust, but when we understood that you finally, really trusted us, it was liberating."

The desire to dance had forced me to loosen my grip on the agency. In turn, I had learned that other people had their own wisdom and knowledge to contribute to the success of an enterprise. Moreover, by insisting that I needed to be solely in charge, I had actually been limiting our success to that of only my own abilities, talents, and vision. Yikes!

⁓

The desire to dance had forced me to loosen my grip on the agency. In turn, I had learned that other people had their own wisdom and knowledge to contribute to the success of an enterprise. Moreover, by insisting that I needed to be solely in charge, I had actually been limiting our success to that of only my own abilities, talents, and vision.

⁓

One of the first lessons I had learned in ballroom dancing was that having a strong professional dance teacher as my partner wasn't enough to win competitions. Having a strong leader-follower partnership was the important thing. Judges on the competition floor can tell if the student in a Pro-Am event is following and responding to her teacher's lead, or if she is attempting to lead the teacher. If she's doing the latter, the team will get penalized. But it's hard not to take the lead when you're used to being in charge.

The first time Tony said, "Will you *please* let me lead?" I was honestly surprised. I wasn't even aware that I was trying to usurp his leadership role. My joking response was, "Oh, *you* want to lead? Okay, you can lead." But it wasn't that simple—Tony and I have had that same exchange countless times over the years. Susan, a friend who also takes lessons from Tony, is a type A personality who works in global finance and manages hundreds of employees. She's accustomed to directing large teams and has told me that what she likes most about ballroom dancing is that she doesn't have to direct anyone. I believe her, but I remember hearing Tony grouse about Susan, too, complaining that female executives are the most difficult students to teach because they have a hard time giving up control. It's true. We can't help it. Once we know what the routine is, we want to just dance the routine rather than follow the lead of our teacher/partner and allow him to lead us through the steps.

There are many reasons that trying to dance the routine on your own without following your partner's lead is a bad idea, aside from the fact that the judges will penalize you for it. The most obvious reason is that it just doesn't work—a couple will look clunky and out of sync if both partners are trying to lead. Another equally important reason a female dancer must learn to follow is so the team can be nimble and flexible in navigating the often-crowded competition space. In the studio, Tony and I could practice until we had a routine down perfectly, but in competition we had to be prepared for the unexpected. This was especially true of the smooth dances, which required us to travel around the entire ballroom floor. It's crucial to any pair's success that the female stays attuned to signals from the man, because you never know when another couple will come twirling right in front of you.

In competition I learned that following is not passive—it's active. I had to be extremely alert and responsive to Tony so that I could instantly react with him to conditions on the floor. He might be looking over my shoulder and see that a couple was going to crash right into my back and I wasn't even aware of it. He'd then have to give me a signal that moved me out of the way, and I would have to follow his lead unquestioningly.

Following *unquestioningly* was another thing I had a hard time doing. No matter what the situation was, public or private, I needed other people to make a case for why I should do what they wanted me to do. But when you're on the dance floor, it's like being in the army. You have to do what your commanding officer orders without question or you might endanger your life and that of others. Of course, no one's going to get killed on the dance floor, which means there is considerable temptation for someone like me to resist those orders and think, *I'm going to do it my way, because what's the worst that can happen?* The answer, driven home to me many times, was that we would fumble or miss each other's signals and not dance well or fail to place in the competition when we should have. Then Tony would get irritated with me, especially if he felt that I was a better dancer than the person who had placed ahead of me.

My struggles with being a good follower-partner made competitions interesting for the first few years I was dancing, but I eventually admitted that I had no choice but to succumb. Unfortunately, even when I dutifully followed Tony's lead, there were plenty of heats when we didn't get to perform our routines as we had rehearsed them. Inevitably other couples would get in our way on the competition floor, and when that happened—as it might two or even three times during a ninety-second heat—Tony and I would have to stay in a holding pattern. When the other couple moved, Tony would sometimes have to change the routine in order to make it work depending on where we had to pause and the physical space available to us on the dance floor. To my great annoyance and frustration, it seemed like we *always* had to change the routine. I would be fuming as we left the dance floor, thinking, *My beautiful foxtrot! I couldn't perform the full routine. We only did three-quarters of the routine. And I had to do a couple of the figures that really showed me off in only half the space that I needed because other couples were in our way!* I would get so aggravated that it would affect my next dance, the Viennese waltz. I loved my Viennese waltz, so I didn't want to mess that up, but sometimes I would because I was in such a snit over my truncated foxtrot.

My intense frustration at not being able to control the other dancers felt all too familiar. Having to make maddening midcourse corrections on the dance floor was like a musical version of all the things in my life that got aborted or reshaped—the many events that did not go according to plan. At the time I took up dancing, my whole life was about trying to manage what I thought of as my four worlds—my personal life (including Assad's health), my work, my non-profit commitments, and my dancing. I felt as if had to direct everything and fight to make sure no one changed my plan in any one of my worlds, or else I'd have to reconfigure the entire Jenga-like tower of arrangements.

After Assad died, I had one less thing to manage. That was when I started the process of letting go. It became easier to follow Tony's lead on the dance floor, and easier to see the benefit of letting others lead at work. Naturally I had learned to be resilient in business and to think on the spot, but it was on the ballroom floor with Tony that I learned changing the plan and following someone else's lead was not necessarily a second-best solution. It could be a strategy for winning.

—

I had learned to be resilient in business and to think on the spot, but it was on the ballroom floor with Tony that I learned changing the plan and following someone else's lead was not necessarily a second-best solution. It could be a strategy for winning.

———

That was the attitude I had about our possible deal with Carter Ryley Thomas. Although Mark Raper graciously referred to the arrangement as a merger, it was, in fact, an acquisition. CRT would buy PT&Co., and I would no longer be the CEO. I would have a primary position within the new company, but I would not be the leader. I was comfortable with that. However, Ellen, Evelyn, and Maria weren't so sanguine. They wouldn't be able to work with complete autonomy any-more, and that prospect made them extremely anxious.

A few months after Mark Raper first suggested the merger, I got a chance to put partnering into action on a large scale. I didn't do it to show the others how well a partnership could work, but it ended up being an excellent case study for that. The client was the wine industry in Spain's Rioja region. "La Rioja" specializes in red wine, which it has been producing since the eleventh century BC. With about six hundred bodegas, or wineries, it is the oldest and most prominent of Spain's wine regions. Yet unlike Napa Valley or the wine regions of France, in 2004 Rioja was virtually unknown to North Americans, especially Generation Xers and millenials who represented future wine drinkers. The Consejo Regulador de la Denominación de Origen Calificada Rioja, which is the trade association that represents the region's wineries and grape growers, wanted to hire a PR agency to raise Americans' awareness of wines from Rioja, Spain.

In vying for the Wines from Rioja account, PT&Co. was up against the biggest of the big agencies as well as several small PR boutiques that exclusively represented individual wineries and wine regions. What would be the best way to compete against those two extremes? My solution was to do what I knew the big agencies were not willing to do and the small agencies didn't have the resources to do: partner with a brand consultancy to offer a comprehensive, integrated marketing campaign that involved advertising, digital marketing, PR, sponsorships, and events. The reason the big PR agencies wouldn't want to do it was because they would have to scale their fees down too much to accommodate other non-PR elements in the campaign budget. The big agencies, I surmised, would probably propose a PR-only program, which would net them more fee—possibly as much as 70 to 80 percent of the total budget. I believed that what was in the best interest of the Wines from Rioja client was an "integrated marketing campaign," not just a PR campaign. To accommodate those non-PR elements, PT&Co.'s fee would have to be limited to around 30 to 40 percent of the total budget. The total Wines from Rioja's budget for the first year was $2 million, and to my way of thinking, 30 to 40 percent of $2 million was a very nice chunk of change. If we could find a partner to handle the non-PR components of this integrated campaign, we could knock out both the small and the large agencies. We found our advertising partner in Jon Stamell, a branding expert who specialized in imported foods and wines. Jon's approach to work and workplace culture was in sync with ours, and we had occasionally worked with him as a consultant in the past. Asking him to be our partner on the Wines from Rioja pitch was a logical step.

The challenge of marketing Rioja wines to Americans was manifold. People didn't know Spanish wines; they didn't know Rioja was a Spanish wine region; they didn't know Tempranillo, the predominant varietal in Rioja wines. They knew Cabernet, Merlot, and Pinot Noir, but they had never heard of Tempranillo. And unlike France, where the wineries were tourist attractions that had been visited by millions of North Americans, Spain had not made its wineries easily accessible to the public. On the contrary, visitors to wineries in Rioja needed to make a special appointment to have a wine tasting. The whole Rioja region was largely unspoiled by commercial tourism, which could be a blessing to adventurous travelers but was one of the challenges in marketing its wines.

Wines from Rioja would be a marketing campaign for a region, not for an individual brand, so everything we did had to promote the region. Like most Americans, our new business team was not very familiar with the Rioja region and its location or its wines, so we conducted extensive online and off-line research, talked to wine writers and wine retailers familiar with the region, read books about Spain, and even rented *Silencio Roto*, a 2001 film shot in the area. The lush, mountainous landscape in the movie looked much different from the dry southern coastline most Americans imagine when they think of Spain.

Our research revealed that Rioja's culture was sophisticated (in part because of its prosperous wine industry), convivial, and centered around socializing with family and friends. Good food and wine were naturally the focus of these gatherings. The landscape of Rioja was lovely, full of rolling vineyards set against distant craggy mountains. It looked like Napa Valley, only with medieval villages and castles. Although the region valued and protected its pristine countryside and ancient villages, the wineries had hired world-class architects like Zaha Hadid, Frank Gehry, and Santiago Calatrava to create striking modern facilities. The more we learned about Rioja, the more it became apparent to us that from a PR standpoint the area was a potential treasure. It had everything Americans already loved, but was unknown territory to them—an artisanal locale, if you will.

In addition to generating awareness about the Rioja region, our assignment was to educate Americans about Rioja wines. The decision to partner with Jon Stamell immediately paid off. He had a research firm as a side business, so we mined some of his data to determine which audiences we should target in order to increase awareness and trial—or sales—of Rioja wines in the United States. The vast majority of current wine drinkers, we learned, were the nearly 80 million Baby Boomers. The 40 million Generation Xers were the next largest consumers of wine, followed by millenials, a huge demographic cohort of roughly 80 million who would come of legal drinking age in the next five to ten years. The thing about Boomers, though, was that the older they got, the less they drank. Which begged the question, who would make up the largest volume of Rioja-lovers five or ten years down the line? Clearly we had to direct a marketing campaign to all three age groups.

We knew that the Consejo Regulador wanted the agency to devote 100 percent of the PR effort to targeting Boomers. It didn't make sense to do this when we considered the longer-term sales potential for Rioja Wines in the U.S. market. Our goal, always, was to lay the foundation for creating a long-term relationship with clients. We decided to tackle the problem right out of the gate, and that's what we did when the Consejo Regulador and other officials from Spain visited our office to hear our presentation.

"We want to make sure Rioja is strongly positioned to harvest all the potential wine drinkers that are within the Generation X and Millenial cohorts," we told them. "Obviously, we only want to target people who are twenty-one or older. But in the next five years many more Millenials will be crossing over to legal drinking age. We need to plant the seed that drinking wine is what they should aspire to, not drinking beer or spirits. Drinking spirits was what Generation X did, and Millenials presumably don't want to be exactly like Generation X. Drinking beer is okay at the frat house, but you're not going to impress a woman with your beer-drinking prowess. So there are different ways of approaching each cohort to make wine drinking appealing and then to make wines from Rioja *the* wines to drink."

They didn't seem convinced. While they absorbed the idea, we moved on to the heart of the campaign, which we called "Vibrant Rioja."

"Our goal is to introduce the Old World wine region of Rioja to a new generation of wine consumers in America. Our simple call to action will be, *'I'd like a Rioja.'* We want those words to flow from consumers' lips as easily as *'I'd like a Cabernet.'* The Vibrant Rioja campaign will reposition Rioja as an attainable, sophisticated wine that emotionally connects people to a distant land that's historic and modern, welcoming and passionate. In a word: *vibrant.*" We went on to outline the wide scope of the campaign, which would include consumer and trade relations, marketing PR, strategic food/wine/lifestyle events and sponsorships, website and database development, online and print advertising, retail activities, and branded point-of-sale and other campaign collateral.

Jon was our partner on all the creative brainstorming sessions for the Vibrant Rioja campaign involving both PR and advertising. We partnered closely together in developing every aspect of this integrated campaign and partnered in presenting it to the prospective client as well. My instincts were correct: we won the three-year account. We beat out much larger PR agencies that approached it as a PR-only assignment, and we beat out the boutique agencies because we offered a much more robust, totally integrated marketing campaign.

At the beginning of the campaign, Jon and I acted as comanagers. Then I saw that this arrangement was impeding his ability to get the job done effectively. The staff would respond to his instructions with, "What does Patrice think? Did she approve this?" The comanager experiment was slowing us down. Finally I said, "Jon is the campaign director, and we'll all take our lead from him." For the first time, I relinquished control to someone outside the agency. I gave up the need to be in charge for the greater good of the team, the campaign, and the client. It worked beautifully and was a fine example of how PT&Co. could successfully partner with another entity.

♪

At the same time PT&Co. was enjoying a beautiful partnership with Jon Stamell, my dance teacher and I were having a little power struggle. I wanted Tony to teach me the salsa, and he kept putting me off. The reason I had originally wanted to learn how to dance was so I could do rhythm dances like the salsa and the samba, but because Tony specialized in smooth, he encouraged me to do that as well. He said that learning smooth would strengthen my rhythm skills, and it had. Now Tony and I were working on another rhythm dance, the mambo, and as usual I was having trouble with the beat. It dawned on me that Tony probably didn't want to complicate things by teaching me the salsa, where you danced on a different beat than in the mambo. Finally I thought to myself, *I'll just take lessons from a different teacher who specializes in salsa.* I asked the woman at the front desk of Stepping Out Studios, where we now practiced, if she could recommend a good salsa teacher.

"Emmanuel Pierre-Antoine," she instantly responded.

A few days later I showed up at the studio for my first lesson with Emmanuel. I recognized him as soon as he walked in. I had seen him dance before, about a year earlier at the American Star Ball, where I had competed with Tony. Emmanuel and his then-partner, Alexandra Gregoire, were both from Haiti. Their performance had caused a sensation just short of a scandal. The two of them danced like no one else at the competition, pumping total body-gyrating rhythm into every step and movement. At one point in their routine, they got down on their knees and danced all the way back onto their heels like contortionists—things nobody did in ballroom. Some of it looked like African tribal dancing, some of it looked like hip-hop. It was shocking and borderline distasteful. People in the audience were looking at one another as if to say, "What the hell is that?" I know that's what I was thinking. At the same time, it was electrifying and mesmerizing.

Sometime later I saw a video of Emmanuel and Alexandra doing a Halloween performance in Haiti. Alexandra was wearing a skimpy voodoo priestess costume and Emmanuel was dressed like a Catholic priest. At one point Alexandria stood over him while he lay on the floor writhing and shivering as if possessed, only to spring up a moment later and launch into an explosive performance with her, their frenzied shimmies suddenly punctuated by syncopated, slow-motion gyrations. It was mind-bending choreography.

Obviously Emmanuel wasn't just a salsa teacher. I asked around and discovered that he had risen from very modest circumstances to become one of the top professional American Rhythm dancers. As a young man in Haiti, he had spent eight to ten hours a day practicing and teaching dance while attending university, where he majored in economics and journalism.

In 1997 Emmanuel had founded Caminito, which came to be regarded as one of the leading schools of ballroom and international dance in Haiti. Under his direction Caminito grew to be a school of international repute and import. He organized and choreographed frequent shows and performances and established training and seminars for professional dancers in Port-au-Prince and some of the major provincial cities. Due in large part to Emmanuel's unflagging determination, ballroom dancing (or at least his version of it) was embraced and woven into Haiti's cultural and folkloric fabric.

Emmanuel first captured the attention of the international ballroom world at the 1999 World Mambo Championship in Miami, his first-ever competition outside of Haiti. He and his partner made the finals and took third place, creating a major upset in the ballroom world when they beat veteran ballroom professionals. In 2003 Emmanuel closed Caminito and left Haiti to pursue his dream of a dance career in New York City. He and his new partner, Poland-born Joanna Zacharewicz, were top-ranked professionals in the world of American Rhythm and would soon win the World Mambo Championship.

Emmanuel was a gifted teacher, and I signed up to take two rhythm lessons a week with him while I continued taking three smooth lessons a week with Tony. Their approach to teaching was quite different. Tony was a beautiful, expressive dancer, like Fred Astaire, and also a perennial student, eager to take classes taught by other coaches (all current and former dance champions). He was a sweetheart and a patient teacher. For Tony, dancing was about perfecting the biomechanics and technique—and, of course, the feeling he got when he danced. For Emmanuel dance was spiritual. It was an act of meditation, his way of communing with the divine. He didn't announce this at our first lesson but slowly opened up to me after we had been working together for many months. For him, dancing was the opportunity to be fully present in every moment, and in mind, body, and spirit. The first thing he taught me wasn't a dance move at all, but a new way of understanding the act of dancing.

"In dance, every step *produces* the next step," he said. "Each step is not a separate, disconnected movement, it's the result of your previous step and it *produces* your next step. So if you're focused on fully executing your present step, then you will produce the next step well. You should not get stuck in the past, worrying about the misstep you just made, and you should not jump ahead to the future, worrying about your next step. You just need to stay present and execute your step full-out."

Me dancing rhythm with Haitian-American dance champion Emmanuel Pierre-Antoine. He is always very expressive, which rubs off on me during our performances. When I dance with Emmanuel I can't help but smile.

—

"In dance, every step produces the next step . . . Each step is not a separate, disconnected movement, it's the result of your previous step and it produces your next step . . . You should not get stuck in the past, worrying about the misstep you just made, and you should not jump ahead to the future, worrying about your next step."

—

This was a profound revelation. Until that point, I thought dancing was the act of producing every step independently. I had never taken a dance class before I turned fifty, and I could see that I learned differently from other women my age who had been dancing since they were six. They learned with their body first, not their mind. Because I learned to dance as an adult, I intellectualized my dancing: *I should move this hip, and then this shoulder, and then this knee and this foot.* But dance is not supposed to be an intellectual exercise. You're simply supposed to use your body to imitate the dance your teacher is showing you. I struggled because I was always trying to understand and memorize the moves and then translate them into my body, which was a much less efficient way to learn.

———

Tony often told me, "Stop thinking about it. You're in your head too much. Just dance." Later Emmanuel would say the same thing . . . he often reminds me, dancing isn't about doing each step perfectly. It's about doing each step fully—fearlessly, with conviction, and going all out.

———

Tony often told me, "Stop thinking about it. You're in your head too much. Just dance." Later Emmanuel would say the same thing, but at least by then I understood what was at stake. The secret to beautiful dancing was to totally focus on your present step, not thinking about your last step or your next one. A typical ballroom dance routine is one minute and thirty seconds, and I discovered that this was a long time to concentrate fully on every present moment. To this day, I don't think I've ever achieved it. Emmanuel says no one does. Perfection is never attainable; it's not a destination, it's just a direction you aim toward. Besides, he often reminds me, dancing isn't about doing each step perfectly. It's about doing each step *fully*—fearlessly, with conviction, and going all out.

Being fully present dancing with Emmanuel meant just that. All I needed to do was to stay present and follow him. Not follow my routine, but simply follow his lead, which was exactly what Tony was trying to get me to do, too.

I didn't tell Tony I had hired another teacher, and it hadn't occurred to me that I should. Little did I know that in the ballroom world, having two teachers was very unusual. You were expected to dance all styles with one teacher, which was in part because the teachers (understandably) wanted to protect their income. I was oblivious to the one-teacher-per-student protocol. When Tony found out I was taking lessons from Emmanuel—which he did within a couple of weeks, because the ballroom world has a very active grape-vine—he was a gentleman. He and Emmanuel were friends, and he understood and supported my desire to be an equally strong rhythm and smooth dancer.

As it turned out, taking all those lessons and trying to learn ten different dances—six with Tony and four with Emmanuel—was too time-consuming for me, so after a number of months I told Emmanuel I was going to stop taking rhythm lessons with him for a while and focus on my smooth dances. My intention was to resume my rhythm classes after I had improved in smooth and wasn't so stressed about the impending sale of PT&Co.

It took nearly a year to persuade Maria, Ellen, and Evelyn that merging with Carter Ryley Thomas was our best option, and then to work out all the details. In September 2005, when Mark Raper and I were in North Carolina for a Lumin Collaborative summit, the negotiations had reached a crescendo. Lawyers from both sides were calling us throughout the three-day summit to resolve every last sticking point. Most of the objections were, not unexpectedly, coming from PT&Co. At one point Mark turned to me and asked point-blank, "Is this deal going to happen?"

"It will happen," I assured him. "We'll have a signed agreement before the end of this summit." And, finally, we did.

Mark and I said nothing to the CEOs of the other partner agencies attending the summit because we needed to first go back and share the news with our respective agencies. But that evening over our final group dinner, Mark stood and made a toast. "I know great things will result from this gathering of the minds," he said. Our eyes met briefly, and I nodded my head and raised my glass a bit higher in Mark's direction. I know we both drank deeply at that point.

When the ink was dry on the merger agreement, Ellen, Evelyn, and I were cautiously optimistic. Maria couldn't muster more than resignation. Like me, she didn't always do well with change, especially of this nature. But even Maria could see we had no better solution. The slow drip of declining business was too painful and disheartening. We all wanted to give the agency a fresh start.

One thing was undeniable: we now had a really good reason to throw our fifteenth-anniversary party. We all agreed that a pre-Halloween party in October would be the ideal place to celebrate our years at PT&Co. and to announce the creation of our new combined agency, which would be called CRT/tanaka. It so happened that Emmanuel and Joanna had just won the World Mambo Championship in early September at the U.S. DanceSport Championships in Orlando. I was thrilled for them and the thought popped into my mind, *Why not hire them to do a mambo performance at the anniversary party? They could teach everyone how to do the mambo, too.* I knew how electrifying and high-energy their performance would be, and on a slightly less conscious level I also knew that this would be a coming-out party for me. Aside from people at the agency and my close friends, no one knew about my other life as a ballroom dancer.

I had been dancing for about two years by then, and my physical appearance had slowly evolved. The most obvious change was my weight. I had shed twenty-five pounds, and on my four-foot-ten-inch frame, that was a lot. It wasn't only the exercise that had caused me to slim down, but also my desire to look good in my dance costumes. Knowing that I had beautiful gowns to wear and judges to impress was a powerful motivator. My formerly short, sleek, black hair was now shoulder length and brown with blonde highlights. I had finally ordered contact lenses—my chunky, black-framed glasses were history. And all the hours I had spent perusing the booths at dance competitions had definitely affected my taste in clothing and jewelry. For the party, I wore a sleek, brown silk and satin cocktail dress and a bronze collar with brown stones, and earrings to match. As a colorful and dramatic accent, I wore an acid-green, bronze, and brown satin wrap around my shoulders. My hair fell full and loose with big curls onto my shoulders. I felt like a glamorous, exotic creature—part real world and part ballroom world. When Evelyn saw me that night she said, "You look like a butterfly emerging from her cocoon."

We booked Lotus, a trendy cocktail lounge in the hot Meatpacking District near our office, for the "Mamboo" party ("mambo" and "boo," for Halloween). Invitations went to all our family, friends, and work acquaintances. About 350 people helped us celebrate that evening. It was a high-energy affair attended by many clients and business partners of both PT&Co. and Carter Ryley Thomas, who wanted to share in the celebration with mojitos, mambo music, and much dancing. Our longtime designer, David Lees, who in a former life was the in-house event designer at Studio 54 and helped PT&Co. create many memorable special events, brought the party to life in Lotus Lounge with neon "Mamboo" signs that glowed in the dark, pulsating in hot pink, yellow, and orange. The room had a distinctly South Beach Latin vibe.

At one point during the evening, Evelyn, Maria, Ellen, and I each made brief, heartfelt remarks about our work together, our great pride in building PT&Co., and our excitement about by joining forces with our friends at Carter Ryley Thomas. Mark Raper, who would be CEO of the new agency, spoke about our adventure ahead and thanked everyone for getting us to this point. Many new colleagues from our headquarters in Richmond, Virginia, flew up for the party. It was fun to be doing steps, turns, and spins on the dance floor with these new playmates in our now bigger "sandbox."

Emmanuel and his partner, Joanna, took to the dance floor and captivated the audience. He, black and beautiful from Haiti, and she, a ravishing blonde from Poland with long, straight tresses, made a striking duo. They performed the cha cha, rumba, bolero, and their World Mambo title-winning dance presentation. I don't think many in the audience had ever seen ballroom dancers up close in their rich, beautifully stoned, body-hugging costumes, and they were mesmerized. Between their electrifying dancing and their theatrical costumes, Emmanuel and Joanna brought the ballroom world into the real world at Mamboo.

For me, the night was a cosmic convergence. Many guests pulled me aside and asked, "Who *are* those people?" I got the chance to explain that they were World Mambo champions and I was taking ballroom dance lessons from Emmanuel. The typical response, especially from business associates, was astonished fascination. "Really? You do this ballroom dancing thing? You get dressed up like your teacher and his partner?" For people who had only known me in my hard-driving PR mode, it was a little mind-boggling.

I remember seeing Jeff Wilson, one of my new Richmond colleagues and a gentle-mannered African American, watching the performance with eyes wide-open and raised eyebrows. I don't think he'd ever seen anything like Emmanuel and Joanna, and certainly not at a business function. Later, when Emmanuel and Joanna were giving mambo lessons to some of the more adventurous party guests, Jeff stood off to the side, wearing the same wide-eyed expression. But within an hour I saw him on the dance floor vigorously shaking his stuff with the other revelers. *Dancing together is an auspicious beginning for our new agency*, I thought, watching Jeff shimmy alongside one of his Richmond colleagues. *Maybe we'll be able to mambo right into our new routine at CRT/tanaka and barely miss a beat.*

INTERMEZZO

Mambo

MANY DANCERS STRUGGLE mightily with the mambo. There are only four numbers to keep up with, but never have four numbers been so tricky. Yet once you master its rhythm, the mambo satisfies. The Cuban-African mother of the cha cha, the mambo is the spiciest of the American Rhythm dances. The highly syncopated, often frenetic mambo sound is distinctive, featuring Cuban instruments such as conga, bongo, claves, and timbales, along with big band instruments such as trumpet, saxophone, and bass.

To get the idea, think of that classic exercise in Italian kitsch, "Mambo Italiano": "Hey, mambo! Mambo Italiano!" On the first beat of music ("Hey"), you do . . . nothing. You hold; you wait. Your ribs and hips may undulate, but your feet must stay still. Many a novice dancer hears the strong first beat of music and moves. The dance instructor patiently explains that you must wait on the first beat. The beginner accepts this dictate with her head—as an intellectual proposition it's pretty simple—and believes in her heart that she is waiting until the second beat to move, but in her eagerness or nervousness, her body moves before the first beat is fully over and the second beat has arrived. Or maybe she misses beat two and moves somewhere around three! Gah! Try again!

The second step is a quick step to a single beat of music, but wait, not *too* quick. It is followed by the three count, which is also a quick step to a single beat of music. Then comes the four, which restarts the nightmare for the nervous beginner. It absorbs the nonmoving one count of the next measure, meaning the four includes the one and covers two beats of music. So the four, together with the one that follows it, becomes a slow step. The count goes like this: hold; two, three, four-hold; two, three, four-hold; two, three, four-hold. Got that? Well, probably not yet. It takes time.

Musician Perez Prado introduced the mambo to a Havana nightclub in 1943, and by the end of World War II, it was all the rage in New York. The mambo spread across clubs, hotels, and resorts, wherever eager dancers wanted to blow off steam and make night raids across the boundaries of socially acceptable sensuality. In the movie *Dirty Dancing*, Jennifer Grey's character, Baby, blossoms from unformed innocent to woman, mostly by learning the mambo from her swoon-worthy instructor, played by Patrick Swayze. Mambo hips employ plenty of Cuban motion, although it's sharper and more twisting than in the romantic rumba, which allows more time for a sensual roll. Steps must remain small to keep up with the snappy tempo. Mambo feet move in sharp, staccato movements. Swivels and fast spins can leave you breathless.

With so much to offer the persistent student, why did the mambo, enthusiastically embraced by an adoring public, fall out of popularity so fast? The new kid on the block, the cha cha, was quite simply easier to count! One, two, three, four and one, two, three, four and one, two, three, four … Each number and the word "and" represents a step. No waiting to move and wondering about the elusive start on the two.

Yes, the cha cha is easier. But for a hot and thrilling dance floor challenge, there's nothing like the mambo.

CHAPTER 8

You Must Be Present to Win: Going with the Flow and Celebrating Success along the Way

"Dance first. Think later. It's the natural order."

—Samuel Beckett

Although neither Carter Ryley Thomas nor PT&Co. had been involved in an acquisition before, Mark Raper and I both assumed our merger to form CRT/tanaka would be relatively easy because our agencies were such a good fit. We shared crucial values about workplace community, and equally important, the two agencies had different areas of expertise. PT&Co. had a strong consumer practice, while CRT specialized in health care and corporate public relations. We had no client conflicts, so neither agency would have to resign any accounts. CRT needed a New York presence to be perceived as a national agency, and PT&Co. would benefit from additional offices in Los Angeles, Richmond, and Norfolk that CRT would provide as part of this merger.

Everything seemed to dovetail so nicely that we didn't dwell much on the specifics of the plan for integrating our two agencies. We did have a shared vision: to combine forces in building a PR agency that was better equipped to compete with the biggest agencies for plum assignments. In terms of logistics, one of the things we were most concerned about was protecting the jobs of people at both agencies. As far as we could tell, we wouldn't have to lay off anyone. We were quick to communicate this news to our employees.

~

Everything seemed to dovetail so nicely that we didn't dwell much on the specifics of the plan for integrating our two agencies. We did have a shared vision: to combine forces in building a PR agency that was better equipped to compete with the biggest agencies for plum assignments.

~

In an acquisition, the typical areas where layoffs occur are finance and IT since the companies in a merger each have these departments, and there is no reason to duplicate the efforts. Usually it is the acquired company's finance department that is the one to get axed, and that is what happened in our case—Carter Ryley Thomas' CFO took over that position at CRT/tanaka. A complicating factor for us was that Evelyn Calleja, our CFO, was a partner, so Mark Raper created a place for Evelyn as head of Human Resources—a field in which she had experience.

Complicating factors number two and three: Evelyn was

married to our beloved IT Guy (yes, that was his actual title), Eric Rode, and PT&Co. was a Mac agency, while Carter Ryley Thomas worked on PCs. Mac has since asserted itself as a contender in the workplace, but at the time it was seen as a platform intended primarily for media companies and artists, not for the average business enterprise. We at PT&Co. were not total strangers to PCs. A decade earlier we had handled the consumer launch of Microsoft's Windows 95, even though we were a Mac agency. We actually had to rent a suite of PCs for our Windows 95 account team so they could properly work on the launch campaign. At the end of it all, we had determined that . . . *Macs rule!*

But that was irrelevant now. Nine months after announcing that no one would be laid off, we had to renege. In the war between the Mac and PC camps, PC was going to win. Eric was adamantly pro-Mac and let the Richmond-based IT support team, headed by Mark Owen, a no-nonsense, retired marine, know exactly how he felt without any sugarcoating. They both stubbornly held to their entrenched points of view. The standoff couldn't continue, so we decided Eric had to go and he went with a generous severance. Understandably, Evelyn felt betrayed, and it sent a jolt of mistrust through the ranks of PT&Co. employees. At the beginning of the transition Mark and I should have said, "We'd like to keep everyone on, but the reality is we may have to make some cuts." At least that would have been a more honest conversation. In our desire to do the right thing, and because of our naïveté about the logistics of mergers, we promised too much.

We all forged ahead with the best of intentions in trying to create a combined new agency. Mark formed a new, ten-member Board of Managers that included six of the most senior CRT executives and PT&Co.'s four co-owners: myself as cochair and chief creative officer; Evelyn as executive vice president of Human Resources, which was one of the areas she oversaw at PT&Co.; and Ellen and Maria as executive vice presidents in the Consumer Practice. Our new play-mates were Mark Raper, CEO; Mike Mulvihill, president; Jeff Thomas, CFO; Brian Ellis, executive vice president and then head of the Health Care Practice; Michael Whitlow, senior vice president and head of the Corporate Practice; and Debbie Meyer, senior vice president and general manager of our Norfolk office.

The Board of Managers was excited about being part of a bigger agency with enhanced capabilities and expanded geographic presence. We all liked and respected one another—everyone was smart, funny, and warm. During board retreats and the weekly conference calls Mark organized in an effort to forge unity among the new leaders of CRT/tanaka, we quickly discovered one another's endearing (and less-than-endearing) idiosyncrasies. To facilitate the integration, Mark, Mike, and our Richmond IT support team, Mark Owen and Rob Rossi, spent a lot of time with us in the New York office.

The situation at work was familiar yet new. We were still working in our airy, loftlike West Village office, yet we had to learn new systems for time and account management. The biggest heartburn for legacy PT&Co. employees was the knowledge that we had to migrate to the PC platform.

Despite the early and traumatic departure of Eric, the actual switch was not planned for another year, when PT&Co.'s existing Mac leases would end, so this unappealing future hung over our heads. Connected to that heartburn was that Evelyn now reported to our president, Mike Mulvihill, and the two were like oil and water. Evelyn was a people person used to being her own boss. Mike was not a warm and fuzzy guy, and he could often default to being a policeman when it came to oversight. Evelyn was not used to being policed. She was incredibly self-motivated, a hard worker, and scrupulous about keeping commitments, and chafed at being monitored.

The new order was not as disruptive for Maria and Ellen, although they both felt somewhat demoted, having run their own practice areas at PT&Co. By the same token, it was difficult for some people at legacy CRT who now reported to me as chief creative officer and head of the Consumer Practice, whereas they previously reported to other executives in Richmond. We were all trying to find our place in this new organization, and I think it's fair to say that we all discovered just how hard old habits die. It got so bad with folks saying, "That's not the way we did it at legacy PT&Co. (or CRT)," that Mark banned anyone from uttering the words *legacy PT&Co.,* or *legacy CRT*. He said we are now one agency: CRT/tanaka. Employees were watching and taking their cues from the new Board of Managers, which meant that we had to keep our anxiety tightly under wraps if we didn't want to make things worse.

—

Employees were watching and taking their cues from the new Board of Managers, which meant that we had to keep our anxiety tightly under wraps if we didn't want to make things worse.

—

The cultural differences between our agencies began to emerge almost immediately. Most obvious, but not instantly apparent to me, was the divide between North and South. As New Yorkers, we were accustomed to being very direct—"Yes, I can do that," or, "No, I can't." To our new brethren from the South, saying no was rude. It took me a while to understand that the New York office was being characterized as the rude office. This came as quite a shock because PT&Co. had a reputation for being one of the nicest PR agencies in New York—in fact, we were noted for being *un*-New York in that regard.

Then there was the male/female divide. Carter Ryley Thomas was run by three men, and PT&Co. was run by four women. In a perfect world our yin and yang would have complemented each other, resulting in mutual harmony and balance. In real life it pitched us into a struggle for the soul of CRT/tanaka—the "big-picture" men versus the "God-is-in-the-details" women. The way we saw it, CRT had wanted to get bigger, so it acquired PT&Co. without giving adequate thought to *why* it was so well respected. At PT&Co., we had always prided ourselves on our attention to detail. When creating a campaign, not only did we carefully consider every strategic and creative possibility, we also made sure the execution was meticulous. For us, growth was never the be-all and end-all. Yes, we wanted to be bigger, but we didn't want to cut corners in order to achieve that. Our vision was to be recognized for having the best workplace and doing the best work. The result was that PT&Co. was a stronger, better-known brand than CRT, which was why the acquisition happened in the first place. CRT was more profitable because, although it, too, had a strong focus on workplace culture and creating great work, its leaders understood the importance of the bottom line and didn't overservice their clients.

The clash between our different approaches to business was most painful (to us) in the way new accounts were handled. At PT&Co., we had a senior person heading every account team and involved in the day-to-day decisions of that team. We believed that if you made the wrong decision at the foundational level and built on those assumptions, at the end of the day you would be building on a faulty platform. In our view, senior input on every decision was the only way we could guarantee the highest-quality campaign and implementation. I had always insisted that if we took on eighteen assignments, we were going to hit it out of the park eighteen times, regardless of whether the client paid us $10,000 a month or $100,000. That was how we retained very loyal clients. It was also why it was hard for us to be profitable.

When we were acquired, profitability became key. One way for agencies to be profitable is to push the work down to more junior employees, which is what Evelyn, Maria, Ellen, and I were instructed to do because, at our senior level, we were more hands-on than we should have been on a day-to-day basis. At Carter Ryley Thomas and most large PR agencies, senior people pitched and won new business and developed the PR strategy and plan, and junior people implemented them.

♪

"Having junior people run accounts is insane," Maria darkly warned us. I couldn't argue with her, but there was nothing to do except try it CRT's way and wait for the results, doing our best to maintain PT&Co. standards where we could. What we perceived as horrifying sloppiness (say, typos on a campaign PowerPoint that boasted about our "flawless execution"), Mark, Mike, and Brian tended to view as no big deal. I had always divided the world into two types of people, those who were "accurate" and those who were "approximate." None of us wanted to be part of an approximate gang that couldn't shoot straight. However, we also didn't want to come across as detail-obsessed females who couldn't see the big picture.

No one at PT&Co. was prepared for how wrenching the transition would be. It seemed that every day we had to adjust to some new way of operating that rubbed us wrong.

Maria found the first year especially grueling. She couldn't help worrying about what might happen two, three, or ten moves ahead on the chessboard, and she saw disaster looming in every direction. After having worked with my partners for fifteen years, I loved them the way you love your siblings.

—

No one at PT&Co. was prepared for how wrenching the transition would be. It seemed that every day we had to adjust to some new way of operating that rubbed us wrong.

—

Even so, I couldn't completely buy into all their angst over CRT/tanaka's growing pains. One thing that affected my perspective was having lost Assad and having seen all he'd gone through. When PT&Co. began talking with Mark Raper in September 2004, my husband had been gone for little more than a year. When we were faced with some exasperating directive from our headquarters office in Richmond, I couldn't help but recall the grace with which Assad had dealt with his illness. For more than seventeen years he endured three surgeries and many postoperative treatments. During one eighteen-month period he was on a continuous infusion of a nontoxic chemotherapy delivered by a pump housed in a shoulder bag he had to carry everywhere. Throughout the day he had to change the dressings and tubing. My husband never said, "I can't believe I have to do this," or even, "I don't feel good." Looking back on how he had handled those seventeen years, it was clear to me that each of us decides how we will experience our lives. We can make it difficult on ourselves or we can make it easier.

Each of us decides how we will experience our lives. We can make it difficult on ourselves or we can make it easier.

The key, I came to learn, was to stay present. It was Emmanuel who had opened my eyes to that. I found myself urging my former PT&Co. partners, "Let's try to make the best decisions we can in this moment. If we get upset about every directive from Richmond, we'll expend all of our energy being angry." We all knew that to a certain degree we were needlessly twisting ourselves into knots. "Just breathe," we would tell one another when someone started to get revved up. Breathing helped us pull ourselves back to the present. Or, we would use our favorite in-the-moment mantra: "Let's jump off that bridge when we get to it."

♪

The other force that kept me relatively sane during the first year of the CRT/tanaka integration was, of course, my dancing. In January 2006 I decided to start taking lessons with Emmanuel again. Watching Emmanuel and Joanna perform at the Mamboo party had reignited my passion for rhythm, the style that had originally lured me into the studio. I loved how Latin music and dances like the cha cha, rumba, mambo, and samba made me want to move my body to the beat in a way that was so earthy, sexy, and soul-satisfying. Just a few months after the Mamboo party, I saw Emmanuel at the Holiday Classic Dance Competition in Las Vegas, where Tony and I were competing. I danced poorly at the event, in part because I was overtired and stressed by all the issues related to integrating both agencies.

"I'm really frustrated with my progress right now," I confessed to Tony. "I've decided to take a break from competing. I'm just going to take lessons with you and Emmanuel."

Tony was philosophical about my decision. "Don't say you're not going to compete anymore," he advised. "Just see how it goes."

Whether I was dancing with Tony or Emmanuel, my biggest problem was always the same: I was afraid of being late for my next step, so I would rush the current step and ruin it, therefore failing to create the right movement to produce the next step and ruining that as well. The vicious cycle was incredibly irritating.

"Focus on the present step, and do it full-out, because your present step is what's going to produce your next step," Emmanuel reminded me.

"I know that in my head, but it's so hard to do," I moaned.

"You need to fully inhabit your mind, spirit, and body in every moment to be fully present," he said, adding, "This is true not just of dancing, but of life."

His words were striking a deep chord. I had always thought that being fully present meant being mindful—that is, being aware of my surroundings and opening my heart to the other people in the room. It had never occurred to me to be present in my body. For many years I had totally disregarded my physical self. That's why dancing had become so important to me. Emmanuel was saying that I could not be fully present if I wasn't present in body as well—hearing and feeling the music not just with my mind but also with my body and soul, and responding to it with all of me so that I could use my body to express my emotions through dance. To do that, I needed to fully inhabit, accept, and even love my body. Not tolerate it or excuse it or work on it, but love it. My reflexive response to videos and photos of myself dancing had always been, *Oh, God, no. I hate having my picture taken.* But there was no way I could "be present" in my body if I had that attitude about it. Part of me would always be recoiling from myself.

Could I consciously decide to change the way I felt about my physical self? I started watching myself more often in the studio mirror when I was dancing, and I forced myself not to automatically criticize my looks or my movements. I had lost twenty-five pounds through my dancing and was receiving compliments on my slimmed-down body from other dancers at the studio. I allowed myself to revel in my rediscovered femininity and started dressing in a more body-conscious way, introducing color and even ballroom jewelry into my business wardrobe. In short, I began dressing like a woman who loves herself and believes she's beautiful. When people complimented me on my style I simply replied that I did it to "amuse" myself.

I allowed myself to revel in my rediscovered femininity and started dressing in a more body-conscious way, introducing color and even ballroom jewelry into my business wardrobe. In short, I began dressing like a woman who loves herself and believes she's beautiful.

I received a lot of attention for the new me. I was neither young nor a conventional beauty, but total strangers would frequently tell me, "You look fabulous!" Thanks to

Photo by Albert Parker, Parker West Photography

I love dancing rhythm—the energy level is so high coming off the dance floor it circulates through the audience, which makes the whole ballroom seem like it has a life of its own.

ballroom dancing, I never went out in public looking sloppy or disheveled. I had a dancer's pride in my appearance. Tony and Emmanuel had both drilled into me the importance of standing tall, keeping my vertical line, and holding my head high no matter where I was.

A watershed moment came early one morning when I was waiting for the elevator in my apartment building. The doors opened and I stepped in. One other passenger was already inside.

"Are you a dancer?" the man asked as the elevator doors closed. I wasn't dressed in my practice clothes, nor was I wearing dance shoes. At four foot ten, my physique didn't exactly shout "dancer."

"What makes you think that?" I asked.

"The way you carry yourself and the way you stepped into the elevator," he replied.

Wow. My training showed even when I wasn't on the ballroom floor. "You're right," I said. "I am a dancer."

♪

While I was taking lessons with Emmanuel, one of my best friends, Julie Zirbel, came to stay with me. Julie had headed up PT&Co.'s Los Angeles office for seven years. When she visited from LA, she would sometimes comment on the intensely masculine atmosphere of New York City public relations and how it was a good thing I possessed, as she put it, "a healthy dose of animus," in reference to Carl Jung's expression for the masculine part of a woman's psyche. I had told her about my dance lessons, but she had never seen me dance in person, only on a website called SambaGrl (www.sambagrl.com) that I had created to post some of my dance videos and share my passion with friends. I was eager to show Julie my latest routines and introduce her to Emmanuel, about whom she had heard so much. After the lesson, I shamelessly prodded her for compliments.

"Pretty impressive, aren't I?" I joked. "I bet you never thought you'd see me shake my booty like this."

"Never," she agreed. "Dancing has definitely changed you over the past couple of years. Don't take this the wrong way, but you seem softer."

"I take it as a compliment," I said.

"But how has it affected your work? Has it been hard to combine SambaGrl with Ayatollah Tanaka?"

"Not really," I said. "It happened slowly. I gradually realized that I don't have to try so hard. I don't have to push and prove every single point. I can be softer and let things flow, and direct them in a positive way, rather than forcing everything. It works out, somehow."

"Maybe because of your reputation and the agency's track record," she offered.

"Right, but before I got into dancing, I could never relax about that or rely on it. I think that, because of ballroom dancing, I got more comfortable with the feminine side of myself, the side that can really tune in to other people, be receptive, and then instantly use that information."

"It sounds like old-fashioned female survival skills," Julie remarked.

"True. In the past, women had to use those skills to influence the men in their lives because they had no other form of power. So naturally, when we weren't forced to do this and could just take power like guys, we went for it. But if you have *both* strategies at your disposal—the 'animus,' when you need it, as well as all the 'female' receptivity and communication skills that the ballroom brings out—you suddenly have a big advantage. When I was younger I wouldn't have known how to make the best use of my feminine side in business, plus I would have been worried about appearing weak. I wasn't ready for it, but now I am."

In addition, the simple fact of feeling more beautiful made me embrace and accept myself and that translated into being more relaxed and exuding more confidence. At work, this new me was just as effective as the Ayatollah Tanaka version, and a lot more fun to be around.

It's not an exaggeration to say that all this was inspired by Emmanuel's spiritual approach to teaching dance and by his constant reminders to stay focused on the present moment in body, mind, and spirit. His religious training obviously influenced his understanding of life and dance. "I want to extend the universe through my dancing," he confided to me. "I'm not a performer—I'm a creator, an artist. I don't need to write down my goals. I am the goal."

He also told me, "The universe knows no time and space. Time is about ego. Your mind lives in the past and in the future. Your soul lives in the present. In dancing, it's your mind that thinks about your missteps, which is the past, and worries about your next step, which is the future. Only your soul can keep you firmly in the present."

—

"Your mind lives in the past and in the future. Your soul lives in the present. In dancing, it's your mind that thinks about your missteps, which is the past, and worries about your next step, which is the future. Only your soul can keep you firmly in the present."

—

With three hour-long lessons a week, I had a lot of time to talk with Emmanuel. We knew each other well, having danced together for nearly a year before my hiatus, and now I was soaking up every bit of his dance wisdom and technique that I could. Still, I was surprised when after only a few months into our new lessons he commented, "The New York Dance Festival is coming up in February. We should compete in that."

"But I don't even know all the new routines you've choreographed for me," I objected.

"Don't worry. You know them well enough."

"I do? Well, okay. Why not?" I didn't particularly want to compete, I just wanted to take lessons, and I was enjoying myself so much that I didn't need anything more. But if Emmanuel thought we could do it, I was game.

Truth be told, one reason I was willing to give it a try was that I had a new peacock-themed rhythm costume. It was over-the-top and much more theatrical than any costume I had owned before. I had asked Kristina Staykova, a professional Latin dancer and inspired designer, to create something that would bring out my inner ballroom diva. When she revealed her creation, at first I wasn't sure whether I thought it was stunning or tacky. The dress was black, form hugging, and brilliantly stoned in different shades of blue, green, and yellow that formed ornate patterns at the neckline, the deep V back, and the hem. A peacock-green flounce, dripping with peacock feathers, created volume all around the deeply scalloped hemline. The same peacock-green flounce and feathers hung from both my wrists. On the dance floor, the flounce and the feathers exaggerated my every wrist, arm, and body movement, which was just fabulous.

I was excited about my costume and competing with Emmanuel in rhythm for the first time, and I wasn't stressed like I usually was at competitions. I had already released any expectation of winning placements because I barely knew the five routines Emmanuel had choreographed for our cha cha, rumba, swing, mambo, and samba.

Before the first heat of our first dance, he whispered, "Just stay present and follow my lead. That's all you have to do." I had no choice, since I wasn't totally sure of the steps in my routines. So I focused on being present and available to following Emmanuel's lead. I messed up my first dance, the cha cha, within moments and just laughed about it. Normally, I would have tortured myself.

When we placed first and second in all of our early dance heats, I was surprised. As the day progressed and we kept placing first or second in most of the twenty-one rhythm heats we danced, I was astounded. The biggest shock came at the end of the day, when we heard our names called as winners of the Bronze Pro-Am Rhythm Championship. I couldn't believe it! Winning was the farthest thing from my mind when I decided to enter this competition—my only goal was to have fun. Standing in the spotlight, smiling hugely and gripping my trophy, I couldn't help thinking of the Girl Scouts and the promise I had made them to win a championship. It had taken four years, but I had finally done it!

I watched the video of our performance afterward, fascinated to see what our winning routines looked like, especially the parts where I had forgotten my steps. Missteps happen in a split second, but you can quickly recover with your teacher's help as long as you don't flash a big sign of dismay on your face announcing, *I really messed up and forgot my routine*, which is what I usually did. This time I was having so much fun that I was laughing when I forgot my steps, so no one noticed.

By now I had a stack of competition videos that my teachers and I used to pinpoint ways I could improve my dancing. Every so often I'd look at some of my earliest competitions just to see how far I had come. They reminded me of the saying, "Anything worth doing is worth doing badly."

When I first started ballroom dancing, it was not a pretty sight, but I kept doing it because I loved to dance. Because I'm a perfectionist, my mistakes had really bothered me. I would watch them again and again like painful replays of ABC's *Wide World of Sports'* "agony of defeat" skier mishaps. But the curious thing about scanning the competition videos for my mistakes on the ballroom floor was that sometimes it was very hard to detect them. Often that was because the floor was crowded with other couples and the only people who knew our routines were me and either Emmanuel or Tony. It occurred to me that if I couldn't spot my errors on the videotape it was doubtful the judges would have seen them unless I happened to be dancing directly in front of them. The times I could most easily spot my missteps were when I failed to continue dancing. In addition to revealing a big expression of surprise and dismay, I would stop dancing for a split second in acknowledgement of my misstep, which then messed up my next step. At those times, I saw that the judges would be more apt to notice that I had made a mistake.

At one ballroom competition about a year into my dancing career, I had made so many errors in my mambo that I left the floor grief-stricken, certain I wouldn't win a placement. I ended up receiving a first place for that mambo, and I got so angry that I told Tony I wanted to return it because I didn't deserve it! After he stopped laughing, he tried to explain that placements weren't conferred based on a dancer not making any mistakes. They were based on the quality of the dancing. Quality meant your commitment to the dance as well as the way you moved. At the time I didn't believe what he was saying because I was fixated on how "imperfectly" I had danced my mambo. I was outraged that the judges didn't see my mistakes and judge them appropriately. Now I understood.

♪

Stay in the present and dance through your mistakes—I had a trophy to prove this was a winning strategy. Soon I would have the opportunity to test it at work. The newly merged CRT/tanaka team was meeting with a group from Charles Schwab & Co. (which had been a PT&Co. client for six years), along with representatives from some of Schwab's other advertising and marketing agencies to brainstorm a financial literacy platform for the company. Reviewing a list of who would be attending this meeting, it occurred to me that there were an awful lot of names on it—twenty-five. Our Schwab client had asked us to secure a moderator in anticipation of the large number of participants in this brainstorm, so we hired a consultant, Darren, with whom we had worked successfully for many years. I trusted that Darren would know what to do if the meeting became unwieldy.

Marcy Walsh, the talented new account manager from the legacy CRT side of the agency, Ellen, and I attended the meeting along with our two Schwab clients, Carrie Schwab-Pomerantz, daughter of Charles Schwab, and Sarah Bulgatz, the thoughtful and cerebral communications director who was our day-to-day client contact.

Because so many of the attendees were new to the client and unknown to one another, there was a lot of preening and posturing. For much of the meeting it seemed that all of the agency representatives were talking but no one was really listening to one another or to our Schwab clients. To compound the situation, Darren, who on many prior occasions had performed his moderator role brilliantly, lost control of the meeting and faded into the background like a schoolboy. It was a hot mess of a failed brainstorm.

Afterward, Marcy and Ellen approached me with some alarm.

"That was a disaster," said Marcy. "And what was up with Darren?"

"I have no idea," I said. "He just threw in the towel at some point. I'm going to call him and ask what happened. I'll also ask him to reduce his fee. But first I'll invite our Schwab clients to our office tomorrow morning for a smaller meeting with just us. Believe me, this is very salvageable."

When Carrie and Sarah arrived at our office the next morning, I briefly apologized for the failure of our moderator to control the previous day's meeting and quickly moved on to the present moment. I knew it was critical that we focus on the client and really listen to her. At the end of an hour, after being fully present and paying close attention to what Carrie said and what she didn't say, and considering what we knew of Schwab and its culture, I understood that Carrie was at a crossroads. She didn't want just another public relations campaign. She had deeper things on her mind, such as her father's mortality and the legacy of the company he created.

Because I was fully present and tuned into Carrie's spoken and unspoken desires, I was able to devise a solution for them right there on the spot. What Schwab needed was a credo, similar to the Johnson & Johnson credo written by the company's former chairman, Robert Wood Johnson. That one-page document institutionalized J&J's business ethos and philosophy.

"Schwab could design a credo building on its already strong record of ethical customer service, and expanding over time to include more philanthropy, consumer education on financial literacy, and corporate social responsibility initiatives," I suggested.

I quickly sketched out a schematic to illustrate the multi-year path for Carrie and Sarah. I later named this vision for Schwab "The Schwab Compact" (inspired by the Mayflower Compact) and described it as an ongoing commitment to strengthening America's financial constitution. Carrie was thrilled to have a way forward that built on what her father had instinctively done simply because it was the right thing to do. She left our office that day very happy.

Over the course of my career I had salvaged many bungled meetings, but in the past I had always apologized too much and wasted time fretting over my mistakes—a side effect of my perfectionism, no doubt. It was only after winning my rhythm trophy that I truly grasped how much control we have over the way other people perceive our errors, or whether they see them at all. I put this knowledge to use in all my meetings from then on, apologizing sincerely but briefly if we were responsible for some mistake, and then swiftly moving to the present moment.

—

It was only after winning my rhythm trophy that I truly grasped how much control we have over the way other people perceive our errors, or whether they see them at all.

—

♪

Both Tony and Emmanuel consistently reminded me of what I had achieved as a dancer and forced me to stop and acknowledge my successes. Emmanuel was always pointing out, "You couldn't do that six months ago." My automatic response was to think, *If I was really good I would have been able to do it much more quickly* (fretting over past "failures"), or, *Fine, fine, now what's the next routine?* (leaping ahead to the future). My teachers knew that an essential part of the learning curve was to stop and celebrate every one of a student's achievements.

This crucial aspect of learning was brought home to me about a year into the transition. After several excruciating months, our CRT/tanaka Board of Managers had decided that hoping for natural synergy was probably not the most effective way to move forward, so we worked together to create a Strategy Map that would combine the best approaches from both legacy agencies. It was our attempt to put our business plan on a single sheet of paper—if there was one thing I had learned over my career, it was that nobody reads or continues to refer to a plan that goes on for pages. Three items, in my experience, were the most people were likely to remember. The three key areas our Strategy Map focused on were growing the business, working smarter, and developing our people.

The Strategy Map was a big help to our employees because it clearly spelled out what we hoped to achieve. For instance, to work smarter we would "create stronger expertise within the agency for new media, e-commerce, blogs, and technology." Each area listed specific goals. When we first created the Strategy Map, the Board of Managers had meetings where we ticked off items that had been accomplished and discussed goals that had not been met. Like a lot of managers, we were in the habit of focusing on things that had gone wrong or looking ahead to the next goal, while spending little to no time celebrating accomplishments. We were so focused on getting our new agency on track as quickly as possible that we had left out that crucial part of the learning curve.

Neglecting to acknowledge what we had all achieved was undermining our transition and making an already tense situation worse. It made everyone feel as if little progress was being made when, in fact, the senior leaders on the Board of Managers, as well as the employees, had worked their butts off on this integration. Because we didn't stop to recognize our own accomplishments or those of the staff, employees were constantly complaining to management about the slow pace of the seemingly endless integration process. Everyone felt frustrated and dejected, just like a dancer would if she practiced a routine for months and her teacher never bothered to acknowledge and praise her progress.

—

Neglecting to acknowledge what we had all achieved was undermining our transition and making an already tense situation worse. It made everyone feel as if little progress was being made when, in fact, the senior leaders on the Board of Managers, as well as the employees, had worked their butts off on this integration.

—

As soon as I made this connection, we switched gears and began to spread the word about everyone's efforts and achievements. Mark started sending out company-wide emails whenever we accomplished a goal in one of the three key areas, such as when one group created a client satisfaction program that enabled us to identify relationship issues before they become big problems, and to pinpoint opportunities for the agency to become a better resource to our clients. We also announced our progress at the monthly meeting of the MGroup, the next generation of agency leaders who were a level below the Board of Managers.

To encourage opportunities for employees to relax and socialize with one another, we designated a Cheers Committee in each office to plan social events and outings, such as weekly Belly-Ups at the bar that was a fixture on the ground floor of our cavernous, three-story Richmond office. In the New York office, our Belly-Ups involved going across the street to Art Bar in the West Village for agency-subsidized after-work drinks. The Cheers Committees also planned our Summer Outings—summer afternoons when we would treat the staff to a picnic in Central Park or some other outing for the entire office. And whenever the mercury hit one hundred degrees, the Cheers Committees would dispense ice cream to everyone.

All of these efforts, whether they involved socializing or acknowledging our achievements, were celebrations of the present moment. Once we started to do this consistently, we were able to shift our employees' attention from how slow the integration process was to how much we had achieved together and how much we had in common. Gradually the atmosphere at CRT/tanaka improved and the staff started to feel more relaxed and optimistic. Because the employees were regularly reminded of how far we all had come—including the board—they became much more willing to cut management some slack. Not everyone was able to stay on the bucking bronco for the entire thrill ride that was CRT/tanaka's transition. Evelyn Calleja, our former CFO, left the agency at the end of our first year. Though Mark Raper had tried to create a place for Evelyn as head of Human Resources when CRT's CFO took over Evelyn's job, accounting and finance were her passion and focusing exclusively on HR didn't fully challenge her.

It was a bittersweet parting. Evelyn was my closest confidante, and the person on whom I had most depended as we built PT&Co. Back in 1990, when I interviewed her for the position of controller, we had hit it off so well that she had accepted the job without ever asking about the salary. It was only when she went home and told her sisters about this great new agency where everyone was an owner that she realized she had no idea what she would be earning. She had sheepishly called back to ask about that little detail and to formally accept the job. I knew that I would miss her terribly at CRT/tanaka, but our friendship would last a lifetime.

♪

I had met many of my close New York friends at work or through business—no surprise, since that's where I had spent most of my waking hours. In the time that I had been dancing, however, I had become friendly with some of the other students at the Pierre Dulaine and Stepping Out studios. I noticed that many of the female students had personality traits that were, shall we say, familiar to me. These women were type A, tenacious, willing to work obsessively on a routine, and wildly in love with the way dancing made them feel. Soon after I started taking lessons at Stepping Out, I noticed a confident, curvaceous Italian beauty in her midthirties who would often be leaving the studio as I was walking in. I learned that Jackie Soccodato was also a student of Emmanuel, and we soon struck up a friendship. Jackie was a middle school teacher in Westchester, New York, who had been dancing from the age of two and a half. In her late twenties she took up ballroom dancing after seeing the Ohio Star Ball on television, where PBS presents this most prestigious of all U.S. competitions as "America's Ballroom Challenge." After watching the show, Jackie said to herself, "I want to do that. I *could* do that."

A very goal-oriented gal, Jackie had already earned two master's degrees and was working on a third when I met her. In addition to taking lessons from Emmanuel, she also took them from his former partner Joanna Zacharewicz. She ran every day, did Bikram yoga, and took two Zumba classes a week. That was after a full day of teaching middle schoolers.

I once asked Jackie if she could tell me the single biggest lesson she had learned from ballroom dancing.

"Letting someone else be in control," she immediately replied. Naturally I had to laugh.

"I felt like I had to look perfect in public," Jackie recalled. "I'd argue with Emmanuel about learning a new step in the studio because it was a public arena! I wanted to perfect it in the privacy of my own home first. I ended up wasting so much time and money arguing with him instead of dancing that I finally gave in. Now I don't strive for perfection, I just learn the new step. I laugh at myself when I do badly in practice."

"It's very liberating not to have to be perfect," I agreed.

Jackie was so enthusiastic about ballroom dance that she introduced her fifth-grade students to the "Dancing Classrooms" program founded by my first dance teacher, Pierre Dulaine. Each year, she brought the students to Stepping Out Studio so Emmanuel could coach them before the big citywide competition, which was called "The Colors of the Rainbow." One afternoon I watched as he showed the eleven-year-olds how to refine their swing and cha cha steps. Although Emmanuel can be a tough taskmaster, the kids loved him. They especially loved it when he gave Ms. Soccodato "the hand" (as in *halt!*) when she tried to assist him in the coaching session. Emmanuel is not terribly interested in the opinions of other students when he's coaching.

"My kids will never let me live that down," Jackie laughed later.

Jackie and I didn't spend much time socializing at the studio because we went there to practice and take lessons. We got to know each other better at competitions, where we both partnered with Emmanuel. We would watch each other compete—Jackie danced Latin and I danced American Rhythm, which are usually held on different days. We'd cheer each other on and, after each heat, give each other feedback on our performance and appearance compared with the other competitors on the floor.

Friends from the real world, we both agreed, were fun but distracting at a competition. They came specifically to see us dance and weren't much interested in anything else. As soon as we were finished, they would want to leave the ballroom to have a bite to eat or go shopping or sightseeing. Jackie and I wanted to stick around and watch other Pro-Am couples compete. In the evening, we'd watch the professionals dance, including Emmanuel and his new partner, Liana Churilova, a petite and brilliant young dancer from St. Petersburg, Russia.

Jackie and I loved to get all dressed up when we attended the nighttime competitions. Friends from the outside didn't entirely get it. ("But you're not competing, so why are you wearing those rhinestones?" "Is it okay if I wear jeans?" "It's *how* long?") They'd gape at us as if we were groupies when we screamed out the number on Emmanuel's back to show the judges our support (competing couples are identified by paper numbers on the male partner's shirt). Jackie and I were in our element in the ballroom world, and that's where we really became friends.

Another dancer I came to know and love was Annette Overton McGrath. I didn't meet Annette at the studio but through a colleague, Michael Whitlow, in CRT/tanaka's Richmond office who was a neighbor of hers. I never knew anyone more driven to learn about ballroom dancing. Annette was studying and competing in all four ballroom genres—standard, Latin, smooth, and rhythm. She told me that the moment she took her first ballroom dance lesson, she felt a "surge of joy" through her forty-six-year-old body and was hooked.

At age five, Annette had been captivated by the plastic ballerinas that decorated her birthday cake, and she begged her mother for dance lessons. But her family of very modest means in Roanoke Rapids, North Carolina, couldn't afford them. It wasn't until college that Annette finally had the opportunity to learn modern dance, ballet, and jazz. By the time I met her she had been ballroom dancing for two years and was fiercely passionate about it, devoting three hours a day, seven days a week to practicing.

Annette was a woman of many talents on and off the ballroom floor. For years she had earned her living as a journalist, later turning to fiction when she left work to focus on raising her three children. Two were in high school and one was in college when Annette discovered ballroom dancing. When I talked to her about the forces that drew her to ballroom, and what she got out of it, she thought carefully before trying to explain.

"The most important thing ballroom has taught me is to be fully myself and hold nothing back. There are a few reasons why that's been so profound for me. First, there's my height—five foot eight barefoot, and up around six foot in my beloved heels. And most people would agree that I am a lot more intense than the average woman. In the milieu of the southern suburb, I often felt 'too big' in every way. I had to hold myself down to fit in at all. Even then, it didn't do me much good. The 'burbs have been a lonely place for me—definitely *not* a village.

"Second was marital adaptation. My husband is extremely accomplished in his profession but in private life he's very shy and introverted. To keep him comfortable, I channeled my more sociable nature and over-the-top energy into more solitary pursuits that centered around my home and family: cooking, gardening, decorating, and studying music.

"The third reason ballroom has been such a revelation for me has to do with my career. I've always been a nonfiction writer—a journalist—and for most of my life I loved it. When I wanted to have time to raise my children and accommodate my husband's work schedule, writing fiction seemed the most flexible way to continue to write. Unfortunately, channeling myself down this path for many years turned out to be too confining for the kind of writing I do best, which is nonfiction. I held back from that because it was not convenient for everybody else!

"The place where I felt fully myself for the first time in years and years was the ballroom floor. Dancing gave me such joy. It demanded intellectual, emotional, and physical commitment—all of me!—and if I held back on any front, the dancing fell apart and a lot of the joy drained out of it. Holding back was no longer an acceptable approach."

Reflecting on the changes ballroom dancing had made in her life, Annette told me, "I'm not a different person—I'm just unleashed. I no longer feel any need whatsoever to compress myself. My kids are happy with it. Let's say my husband is slowly adjusting to it."

—

"The place where I felt fully myself for the first time in years and years was the ballroom floor. Dancing gave me such joy. It demanded intellectual, emotional, and physical commitment—all of me!"

—

Shortly after starting to dance, Annette decided to put aside writing and embark on a new career as a ballroom instructor. "I gave up on writing. I felt burned-out and purposeless," she confided. "Writing about dance relit that old fire. Now I see writing as something I can enjoy for a few hours a day and perhaps profit from financially, but I know that the lion's share of my time needs to go to physical pursuits for me to continue to be this happy."

I was intrigued that Annette's discovery of something entirely separate from her longtime vocation was the flame that reignited it, just as ballroom dancing had relit my fire for public relations.

"I feel really alive," Annette concluded. "Just a few years ago, I felt invisible. Maybe I had made myself that way?"

It's impossible to know. But "invisible" is how too many women feel. I felt that way myself before; like Annette, I was lucky enough to step onto a ballroom floor.

INTERMEZZO

The Viennese Waltz

LIKE A MAGNIFICENT, ever-shifting kaleidoscope, a ballroom given over to the Viennese waltz is an unforgettable sight. Remember those classic movie scenes where couples whirled around the dance floor, all the while turning, turning, turning in each other's arms? With every gentleman in white tie and tails, and every lady a slender stem rising from the swinging bell of her sparkling gown, those scenes epitomized a dazzling time gone by. In the same way, the Viennese waltz embodies the ballroom world at its most glamorous and exuberant.

Not for the faint of heart because of its speed, the Viennese waltz requires both poise and endurance. Featuring the same one-two-three count as the regular waltz but almost twice as fast in tempo, the Viennese version requires that the couple have body contact to negotiate the frequent turns without slowing down or pulling apart or bumping against each other in a decidedly ungraceful way. This waltz does not get as much play at modern social dances as the regular waltz, foxtrot, and tango. It's a shame because there are many popular contemporary songs with Viennese waltz tempo—Queen's "Somebody to Love" makes a fine Viennese, as do Kelly Clarkson's "Breakaway" and Seal's "Kiss From a Rose."

Once you master its tempo, the Viennese waltz can teach you a great deal about looking positively regal. Make no mistake—this dance takes work. But it can be done with grace—and in a spectacular outfit, which for many dancers is part of the allure. Beautiful posture is central to a well-done Viennese waltz. If you stretch your spine upward in a long line and allow your skull to balance atop it, your clenched jaw will unlock and your tense shoulder blades will relax and drop back where they belong. Your chest will open up, and in this receptive state you can breathe easier and welcome a partner into your elegantly extended arms.

Correct posture not only looks wonderful, it brings greater freedom of movement to your joints and muscles, because everything is lined up, relaxed, and ready. Tension is the enemy of movement. It's like binding your limbs tightly with rubber bands. You may move, but not much, not exactly when you want to, and not well. Also, excess tension makes you feel much heavier to your partner, even if you are lean as a sylph. Your partner wants to move freely with you, not push or pull you around the floor, especially when the music is quick and the other couples think they're dancing on the autobahn. Adjusting your posture and achieving relaxed alertness with your body can cause your partner to exclaim, "You've lost thirty pounds!"

When both of you are standing tall and moving freely, the Viennese waltz allows you to make your way across the floor without having to think too hard about patterns or how to link them fluidly together, which is always a beginning leader's worst nightmare. The Viennese simply does not have many patterns. You can fly around the floor with only three patterns in your repertoire—reverse turn, right turn, and progressive changes—even at beginning levels of competitive dancing. Unlike in regular waltz, you don't have to worry much about rise and fall or sway, because there isn't time to achieve much from one step to the next.

The American Smooth version of Viennese waltz does allow the couple to come out of each other's arms and enjoy free turns and spirals and sweeping arm gestures called explosions. Unless you dance with a very experienced group of social dancers, you may not see many of these open patterns. Tune in to *Dancing with the Stars* or attend a ballroom competition to experience the ultimate in the expressiveness that this fast-moving, magical dance can offer. Tiaras optional!

whatcanbe:
Leading with Your Heart

"On with the dance! Let joy be unconfined."

—Lord Byron

*E*mmanuel often told me, "It's when you're not dancing that you take care of your dancing." He meant that much of what a person does to improve as a dancer happens not in the studio but in the real world. "When you're walking down the street, always hold your vertical line," he said. "Keep your head up and walk with your feet pointing out." If I was conscious of walking that way all the time, it would become a body memory and I wouldn't have to think about it when I was on the dance floor.

I loved the idea of my actions in one world supporting what was needed in another. For most of my adult life I had stacked the commitments in my different worlds into a carefully balanced tower and then fought like hell to keep them from toppling. As I entered my sixth year as a dancer and my second as a partner in CRT/tanaka, I saw that instead of balance, the goal could be alignment—arranging my work, personal life, passions, and community commitments so that they would support and reinforce one another. The key to this, for me, was to let down the wall between my private passion for dancing and my public commitments to the agency and the community. The fact that I had this revelation at the same time we were evolving into a new, larger entity was probably no accident.

I saw that instead of balance, the goal could be alignment—arranging my work, personal life, passions, and community commitments so that they would support and reinforce one another.

My experience dancing had made all the difference in how I navigated the transition from CEO and "leader" to partner and "follower." By the time PT&Co. merged with Carter Ryley Thomas I had won many first, second, and third placements in ballroom competitions, all because I had learned to be a skillful follower. This no doubt helped me to accept, and even embrace, a follower role in my business life. I quickly saw that the merger gave me the opportunity to focus on areas where I excelled and to relinquish responsibility for areas where I didn't. By surrendering the need to be the person in charge, I was free to devote all my energy to what I loved most about PR: creating groundbreaking campaigns.

As CRT/tanaka turned the corner on its first year, I was more determined than ever that we former PT&Co. executives not repeat our past mistakes. I didn't want our new agency to overservice clients or get bogged down in consensus-style decision-making. When Mark Raper told me he wanted to have all fifty employees offer input for our future plans at the agency's yearly retreat, I cautioned, "Let's not." I knew from experience that if fifty people contributed ideas and the final plan didn't reflect all of them, forty-five people would probably end up feeling somewhat marginalized and resentful. Someone had to lead, and others had to be willing to follow.

Just as we at PT&Co. wanted to use past experience to make our new agency stronger, I now could see that CRT's staff was more in sync with PT&Co.'s "God-is-in-the-details" approach than we had originally assumed. They had acquired us because they wanted to find out how we had achieved our outstanding reputation, and they wanted CRT/tanaka to continue that trajectory. Like any marriage, both sides had been a little touchy about territory at first, but our commonalities far outweighed our differences. My first impression of CRT was essentially right: I did like playing in the sandbox with these guys and gals.

Some of my longtime colleagues found new sandboxes to play in. Evelyn and her husband, Eric, started their own company, The Biz Within, which provided financial, IT, human resources, and administrative support for small PR agencies that couldn't afford to hire full-time, senior-level staff in these critical functions. Maria Kalligeros eventually left CRT/tanaka to fulfill a lifelong dream of starting her own agency, Kalligeros Communications. The voluble Frank de

Falco, who had left PT&Co. a few years before the merger, became a PR consultant and also put his encyclopedic knowledge of New York to use by giving walking tours of the city—like me, Frank had found a soul-satisfying passion outside his day job. But petite Ellen LaNicca of the Dyson campaign fame, and the first person I ever hired, remained right down the hall from me at CRT/tanaka. We would often tell new clients that we had been working together for nearly twenty-five years—almost unheard of in the world of PR.

One good omen for CRT/tanaka was that we had lucked upon a brand essence for our new agency before we had even finalized the merger. Lightning struck one afternoon while Mark and I were driving with legacy CRT's then-creative director, Christian Markow, who was telling us about a brand concept Mark had come up with for a client.

"It's called *whatcanbe*," said Christian. "It's about optimism and limitless possibilities."

Christian immediately added, "I think that's a great concept for our CRT/tanaka brand."

"I absolutely love the concept of *whatcanbe* for CRT/tanaka," I said. "And, I think it suits our agency better than it does our client."

In early 2006 we formalized *whatcanbe* as our brand essence. *Whatcanbe*, as we defined it, is a sky's-the-limit approach to life that involves envisioning a bigger, brighter, better future for ourselves, our clients, and our community and then creating a plan of action to get there. The only limitation would be our imagination, and our group had plenty of that. The spirit of *whatcanbe* would be the driving force behind the agency's curiosity, its risk-taking, its focus on creating remarkable solutions, and its commitment to delivering joy and abundance to employees, clients, and the community-at-large.

⌐⌐

whatcanbe, *as we defined it, is a sky's-the-limit approach to life that involves envisioning a bigger, brighter, better future for ourselves, our clients, and our community and then creating a plan of action to get there.*

⌐⌐

A year after the merger, Mark asked that I become the agency's *whatcanbe* ambassador. I would still be at the helm of CRT/tanaka's consumer practice and deeply involved in creating all major campaigns; however, Mark wanted me to help communicate CRT/tanaka's distinguishing brand essence of *whatcanbe* to the outside world while also nurturing this ethos within our own agency culture. I agreed with him that if the *whatcanbe* approach was going to work, it couldn't just be a slogan for clients. It had to be a worldview that all CRT/tanaka employees understood, embraced, and lived. I knew the concept was a little vague to some of our staff, so I created proof points that would help clarify it and at the same time assure our employees that *whatcanbe* was a living, breathing practice at the agency.

Coming up with the *whatcanbe* proof points was a pleasure. First I created a *whatcanbe* task code in our timesheets program to institutionalize the agency's commitment to the concept. CRT/tanaka employees were encouraged to log at least five hours a month to envisioning a more abundant, exciting future for themselves, the agency, or our clients. We provided questions to help spark their creativity: What one thing could I do that might improve success in my personal life, my life at the agency, or the lives of my clients? What one idea would I implement if I were the client? What information could I uncover that might help our clients make better decisions?

Employees who exemplified the *whatcanbe* spirit were honored at our annual *whatcanbe* awards. The winners received a one-week paid minisabbatical and $2,500 to use for a potentially life-transforming experience for themselves—one that needn't relate to the job. In the spirit of *whatcanbe*, an experience that enriched the employee would naturally have a positive impact on all parts of his or her life, including work.

Employees who exemplified the whatcanbe spirit were honored at our annual whatcanbe awards. The winners received a one-week paid minisabbatical and $2,500 to use for a potentially life-transforming experience for themselves.

As we trained ourselves to look for *whatcanbe* opportunities, they began to appear everywhere. For example, when we needed to hire an account manager for our Wines from Rioja client, one of the top candidates was a lovely young woman named Lauren Ray, whose passion apart from wine was health and wellness. At one time she had been a personal trainer, as well as a manager at two top Manhattan health clubs. Lauren also taught yoga and meditation. I told her, "One of the things we're trying to do at CRT/tanaka is build our wellness practice. How would you like to be our wellness director and oversee a wellness program for our employees?"

Lauren was thrilled. She started leading meditation, yoga, and weight-training sessions for our employees, and even made herself available to work one-on-one with them to develop personalized wellness regimens. When potential clients in the wellness community saw our internal commitment to health and fitness, it set us apart from the competition. We're probably the only PR agency ever to be featured in both *Yoga Journal* and *SpaFinders* magazine for our wellness practices. When we could align the passion and interests of our employees and the business goals of the agency, it was a beautiful thing!

As *whatcanbe* ambassador to the world outside CRT/tanaka, I made sure the brand was reflected in every part of our organization, from our business cards (the title "*whatcanbe* ambassador" was a great conversation starter) to our website, holiday cards, and everything in between. I speak about *whatcanbe* at all sorts of professional organizations and even at college graduation ceremonies. It was easy to speak passionately about the optimism and limitless possibilities that were at the core of *whatcanbe*. In the end it was not so different from my mother's rules for living: share your toys and cookies and always treat other people with love, because the more love you give away, the more you will have.

Many of the skills I learned dancing, such as how to be a good follower, were powerful metaphors that I applied to my business life after seeing proof of their value on the competition floor. However, there were some skills that were more than metaphors—they translated directly into greater success at the agency. The most dramatic change had to do with how I communicated. Every ballroom dancer I knew reported that partner dancing had made them more sensitive to nonverbal cues, which is a huge advantage in any business setting.

Dr. Ming Wang, a ballroom friend and Pro-Am champion, once shared with me an insight about the wordless communication that occurs between ballroom partners. "When we watch a world-class couple dancing, the most magical part is not its actual movement, but the split-second before beginning to dance. In that brief, still moment, the partners are sensitive to each other, they respect each other, they communicate, they connect, they feel and understand each other's intention, and they arrive at a combined intention as a couple." My own experience when dancing was that the communication happened before I thought about it. I knew what my partner wanted me to do, but I couldn't really explain *how* I knew. One thing was certain: my new communication skills transformed the way I connected with clients and colleagues.

I had been very goal-oriented my entire adult life. I had to be in order to manage my competing worlds: Assad, the agency (with all its shareholders), and my nonprofit work. My mantra could have been, "Let no extraneous information get in the way of my goal." I usually accomplished what I set out to do, but only at the expense of tuning out a lot of information that could have been important. Maybe that information never got presented to me again. It might have been nothing more than a fleeting expression or slight pause in the conversation, as when Carrie Schwab-Pomerantz wanted to find a way to institutionalize her father's legacy but wasn't able to articulate that desire or to acknowledge her apprehension about a future when her dad would no longer be the guiding spirit at Charles Schwab & Co.

My epiphany—or "Aha!" moment, as Oprah would say—was that the most powerful business communication involves being able to accurately read other people's body language, energy, and oftentimes inchoate desires in order to deliver on expectations they may not be aware of themselves. Ballroom dancing taught me to be more attuned to the personal needs of those with whom I do business—needs that are sometimes more urgent and unmet than their professional needs.

—

My epiphany—or "Aha!" moment, as Oprah would say—was that the most powerful business communication involves being able to accurately read other people's body language, energy, and oftentimes inchoate desires in order to deliver on expectations they may not be aware of themselves.

—

Today if a client hires CRT/tanaka, my position going into the relationship is that I will do anything to make sure the client succeeds. Of course we're going to do a great job for them, but I'm also going to try to make that client's life better for having been engaged with us. If I can see that a client is unhappy, I ask myself, *What could make this person happier?* There is a good chance that a client who is happy in general will be a better client than one who is not.

I'm very aware that public relations can be a subjective art. The same campaign that strikes one person as amazing can strike the next person as just all right. I want every one of my clients to say, "That campaign is brilliant! I love you guys." I want my clients to champion us within their organization. I want them to refer us to other potential clients, and I want their referrals to be glowing. The old-school way of winning your clients' loyalty and enthusiasm (aside from doing great work) was to buy them lunches, dinners, and tickets to ball games or Broadway shows. Those perks are sweet, but they're superficial. They don't make a person happy in any deep, sustaining way, which is what I want for my clients.

My experience with ballroom dancing gave me a framework for talking about possibilities that might improve the quality of a client's life. Judy Blatman, the senior vice president of communications for the Council for Responsible Nutrition (CRN), was one of the first clients I told about my passion for ballroom. At the time we met, Judy was recently divorced. She had no children, so work had become 100 percent of her world, which naturally did not result in a happy client. At our third or fourth meeting, I confessed to Judy that I had been as work-obsessed as she seemed to be, but I had changed my ways. I told her how much happier I'd become after I started ballroom dancing. "My life isn't just centered around work anymore," I explained.

"You're kidding! Really? I used to love to dance."

"Well then, you should dance," I said, and I arranged for her to take a lesson with Tony. She had a fantastic time, went back home to Rockville, Maryland, and started taking ballroom lessons herself. When Judy came to New York a few months later, she confided that she had always fantasized about learning how to sing, too, so she was now taking singing lessons. Judy then fulfilled a longtime dream of attending the University of Iowa's Summer Writing Festival, a weeklong intensive writing workshop. She had always been a wonderful writer, but her efforts had been limited to business. She attended the festival two years in a row and loved it.

By the third year of our three-year contract with CRN, Judy was a much happier person. She was still stressed about her job, but now she had a personal life that made her glad to get out of bed in the morning. Her happiness affected her attitude toward everything, including the work our agency was doing for the Council for Responsible Nutrition. The "Life . . . supplemented" campaign was a success on an objective level, too—in 2010 it won a prestigious PRSA Silver Anvil award, the Academy Award of the PR industry. That same year CRN members cited the "Life . . . supplemented" campaign at a hearing on Capitol Hill as further proof of how the industry was promoting the responsible use of supplements.

Regardless of its success, I was well aware that the campaign required a lot of effort on Judy's part, because she had to raise funds for it from the nearly one hundred member organizations of CRN. When I approached her at the end of our three-year contract with the suggestion that she ask the board to make "Life . . . supplemented" an ongoing effort, rather than a onetime push, we both knew it meant more fund-raising work for her. She was all for it, however, and today "Life . . . supplemented" is continuing onto year four beyond the original three-year commitment by CRN.

Not too long ago Judy remarked to me, "You know, my life has really improved just in the past three years."

"Of course, that overlaps with the time that we've been working with you," I replied, only half joking.

"That's true," she agreed.

It seemed that every week I met new people who were surprised and intrigued when I told them about my life in the ballroom world. Anita Fial, who would eventually sell her highly regarded, food-focused PR agency to CRT/tanaka, was so inspired by my enthusiasm for dancing that she acted on her lifelong fantasy to learn how to tango. She even traveled to Argentina for lessons. Another colleague, who was copublisher of a PR trade paper, confided that she was frustrated at her job, where she felt unchallenged and underappreciated. She was a people person who loved to mingle and entertain. I suggested that rather than look for another position, she hold a monthly salon for women in the PR industry, using her many contacts to establish a name for herself apart from the trade publication for which she worked. She launched the salon soon after our conversation and is still happily hosting this monthly event. Recently, she took this a step further and started her own PR industry trade media company.

The simple formula that had changed my life—outside passion equals happier, more productive professional—seemed obvious now that I was living it. For the first twenty years of my career I had assumed my success was partly due to my talent but mostly due to the fact that I worked harder and longer than anyone else. After ballroom dancing, I came to understand that I didn't need to work so hard. I was getting too old for those punishing hours anyway. Now I felt my energy coming from my optimism and joy, a sense that I could manifest what I wanted less by physically forcing it to happen and more by setting the positive expectation that things would work out for the best.

⁓

Now I felt my energy coming from my optimism and joy, a sense that I could manifest what I wanted less by physically forcing it to happen and more by setting the positive expectation that things would work out for the best.

⁓

Another ballroom benefit that was more than metaphorical was the confidence I gained from being a dancer. This is a common theme among people who learn to dance and the professionals who teach them. John Kimmins, president of Arthur Murray Dance Studios, told me, "Part of the job of Arthur Murray instructors is not only to teach students to dance but also to improve their lives. Dancing induces the confidence that you can achieve something, and that applies to many areas of your life. It makes it easier to have better relations with friends and colleagues."

Ballroom teachers are full of stories about how their pupils blossomed after a few months of dancing. Bob Powers, twelve-year undefeated U.S. National Rhythm Champion (with his wife, Julia Gorchakova), successful ballroom entrepreneur, and developer of the Core Rhythms dance exercise videos, told me, "One of the most rewarding scenarios is when someone who is shy and introverted, who doesn't dress very well and is awkward socially [starts taking lessons], and within a few months is coming to the parties, dancing with everyone, and feeling really good about themselves."

I had never been a shy wallflower, yet ballroom dancing transformed the way I approached public speaking. Because I could compete in front of hundreds of people, including ballroom judges, I am able to give a presentation to a roomful of strangers with greater ease. The knowledge that I had successfully overcome my fear of dancing before an audience makes it a lot easier to address a group about public relations, a subject that I know quite well.

♪

In addition to the poise and confidence I gained from being a dancer, all the hours I spent at competitions taught me valuable lessons about performance. When I watched other people dance, my eyes naturally gravitated to those who danced beautifully and full-out, who were totally involved in creating the dance with their partner, who had a distinctive style and energy, and who engaged the audience. In essence, I was drawn to certain dancers because of the visible joy they experienced in their dancing and their ability to share their joy with the audience. Marianne Nicole, who was (and is) one of the most influential judges in the ballroom world, once told me, "The important thing is to dance with your heart. As a judge, I want to be able to feel your dancing. I want to be entertained. I don't care what your feet or your big toe are doing." And she added, "Leading with your heart is important in business, too."

"The important thing is to dance with your heart . . . I want to be able to feel your dancing. I want to be entertained. I don't care what your feet or your big toe are doing."

I thought about this when I made presentations in my professional life. It started with presenting a campaign I really believed in and cared about, and not being afraid to show the audience how much energy and commitment I felt for it. I stopped worrying about delivering word-perfect speeches. Instead, I immersed myself in the subject matter and then used bullet points to guide my presentation. Rather than speaking to my audience, I engaged them in a conversation. If I was excited about an element of the program, I would stop and tell them, "Now pay attention—this is the really exciting part!"

Being comfortable in my own skin was the reason I could express joy and passion in a business presentation. It was the reason I no longer felt self-conscious or concerned that my delivery might not be perfect or "professional" enough. At times I've even cried in business meetings when I've been moved by extreme passion, frustration, or anger.

The self-confidence went much deeper than physical poise. It went back to what Sam Sodano, former ballroom champion and Ohio Star Ball organizer, had told me years earlier when I asked him what he liked best about ballroom dancing. "It teaches you to love yourself," he had said. Whether I'm on the ballroom floor or in a boardroom, I'm informed by the knowledge that I am a beautiful and loved person. This has contributed immeasurably to my confidence both on and off the floor.

Being comfortable in my own skin was the reason I could express joy and passion in a business presentation. It was the reason I no longer felt self-conscious or concerned that my delivery might not be perfect or "professional" enough.

When Sam shared his insight with me the first year I was dancing, I instantly recognized the truth in what he said. Thousands of dance-hours later, I had a better understanding of why it was true. Ballroom dancing is a sensual and sexually charged activity, and reconnecting with that sexual energy jolted life and passion back into me. The costumes and glamour of the ballroom world inspired me to change my physical appearance, which made me feel better about myself. I lost weight, I grew my hair longer and lightened the color. I traded my glasses for contact lenses. I dared to step away from my black-and-neutral executive wardrobe and embrace some of the colors I loved in the ballroom world—yellow, acid-green, brown, bronze, and gold. My jewelry, once sedate silver, was now bold and colorful, sometimes a little funky and bohemian and sparkly. When I looked in the mirror, the woman I saw was definitely related to the sultry girl in the tangerine tank top who had captured Assad's heart.

photo by Jay Gullixson

LEFT: Me in my standard business attire before the transforming power of dance changed my life.

RIGHT: Me saying a few words at the work "mambo" party. This was the night I totally emerged from my cocoon as a butterfly. I felt so glamorous!

photo by Jacob Blickenstaff, Photographer

♪

By the closing months of 2007, CRT/tanaka had begun to right itself from its wobbly beginnings in September 2005, when two agencies came together with *whatcanbe* dreams of a bigger, brighter, better future. We were growing, adding capabilities and clients, and becoming a strongly integrated new agency. Our clients didn't know about all the hand wringing and angst-filled meetings that took place behind closed doors. We drama queens and kings of PR are nothing if not good actors.

The Vibrant Rioja campaign was the jewel in CRT/tanaka's consumer practice crown. If the fantasy aspect of public relations had been part of its allure to me back in Hawaii, working on Vibrant Rioja was in many ways the fantasy come true. It had started with our tour of the Rioja region in 2005—a visual and culinary extravaganza involving fourteen wineries in five days, a crash course on winemaking in Rioja and Tempranillo (the primary varietal used in Rioja wines), and evening feasts that commenced at 9 p.m. and meandered past midnight. That tour inspired our "Vibrant Rioja" campaign, encompassing PR, advertising, and interactive marketing efforts that involved every platform available at the time, some of which were in their infancy, such as social media.

In addition to time-tested PR strategies such as media relations, press trips, tasting events, event sponsorships, and outreach to influencers in all three age cohorts—Boomers, Generation Xers, and millennials—for the "Vibrant Rioja" campaign we created things like a social media video package on the annual "Wine War" in Rioja, which we posted on YouTube, Facebook, and other sites. Fromager and sommelier Adrian Murcia wrote a "blameitonrioja" blog, and our VibrantRioja.com site provided an evolving source of tantalizing content on Rioja, the wine and the region. Incentives such as a "Rioja wine party for twenty friends" and tickets to New York's Fashion Week 2007 (where Rioja was the officially designated wine) drove traffic to a database of Riojaphiles, which grew to more than seventy thousand names. We hired a Rioja brand ambassador to develop stronger trade relations, including Vibrant Rioja promotions in bars, lounges, and restaurants as well as at retail stores in three key markets: New York, Chicago, and Boston. Looking for even more vehicles with which to promote Wines from Rioja, we partnered with the Culinary Institute of America to send five young rising star sommeliers to the Rioja region, where we filmed an award-winning two-hour educational documentary on Rioja wines that was distributed to more than twelve thousand hospitality and food and beverage directors. It was a long way from my first job in PR pitching stories to the *Honolulu Star Bulletin*!

In December 2007, as our three-year Wines from Rioja contract was about to come up for renewal, *Wine Enthusiast Magazine* named Rioja the "Wine Region of the Year." The Spanish government renewed our contract just in time to celebrate in January 2008 at *Wine Enthusiast*'s Wine Star Awards, a white-tie gala held each year at the New York Public Library.

The awards took place in the library's majestic Astor Hall, a cathedral-like white marble venue with arched bays reaching to a forty-foot vaulted ceiling. Enormous fifteen-foot marble candelabras illuminated the four corners of the hall. Seated at formal tables were 350 movers and shakers of the wine world, their faces aglow from the candlelight and the wine. Our Vibrant Rioja contingent, including many dignitaries from Spain and my partners from CRT/tanaka, filled five tables. I sat at the head table with Victor Pascual, president of the Rioja region's trade association, who had hired our agency three years earlier. He lifted a glass to me and with a heartfelt smile said, "Thank you for getting us here tonight."

"Thank *you*," I said, feeling almost giddy. If only there had been a dance floor, it would have been perfect!

♪

When I started writing this book in 2010, eight years had passed since I first walked into Pierre Dulaine Studio. So many changes had occurred over that time—becoming a dancer, losing my husband, selling my agency. The only things that had remained constant were my weekly dance lessons. Whether with Tony or Emmanuel, those lessons were—and still are—the calm and joyful center of my life.

I love arriving at the studio and seeing couples on the ballroom floor totally focused on practicing their different dances, from the foxtrot to the jive to a wild mambo. I always get a thrill out of seeing the smooth and standard dancers sweep around the floor, navigating in and around the more stationary couples practicing their rhythm and Latin routines. Some couples, connected to a single iPod via earphones, would be performing intimate and intricate partner dances like the Argentine tango, while others took turns using the studio's audio system, playing and sharing their music with the rest of the dancers.

At times the studio's dance floor is like New York City streets—congested with traffic. Emmanuel or Tony and I have to dance defensively, watching out for couples that might move without warning into our space, bumping into us or even smacking one of us with an expressive arm styling. Yes, it can be a little dangerous on the dance floor! But I thrive on the energy of a roomful of couples intently concentrating on their own dancing and not at all self-conscious about practicing in a studio filled with other dancers and onlookers.

My dance lessons are still the only appointments in my week solely focused on me and my pleasure. Although my lessons are not always pure enjoyment—they can be exhausting, frustrating, and humbling—they are also absorbing and joy-filled in that they engage me fully on all levels. I am not distracted or multitasking when I am learning to dance. I am fully present. My two teachers—first Tony, and then Emmanuel—both are passionate about dance, charming and funny, and perfect at mimicking me dancing badly. Their impressions of me are dead-on and usually very unattractive, especially for someone aspiring to dance like Ginger Rogers, but the entertainment factor has been more than worth it. Often I laugh so hard that my stomach hurts, and my hysterical, unladylike guffaws can be heard ringing throughout the studio.

One day the studio manager walked over to me and teasingly said, "You have to stop laughing so much or the other students will expect their lessons to be this much fun, too." It didn't take much to set me off that day because I was already high on joy from my dancing. With every part of my body alive and moving to the music, my joy is always at the surface, ready to break through in peals of laughter at the slightest provocation.

My attitude toward dancing has evolved over the years. Although I am a competitive ballroom dancer (as opposed to a social dancer), I love my dancing so much that it doesn't really matter if I compete or not. In fact, competing is often so nerve-wracking that I prefer my dance lessons and practice to competitions. I compete mainly to monitor my progress so that I can continue to improve.

I am still determined to one day be a Gold-level dancer, moving up from the Silver level that I have now attained. But for me, the true joy of dancing involves learning how to produce a movement with every part of my body to create a dance step or more complex figure. I often spend entire lessons working on just one step, with Emmanuel breaking it down for me as to what my feet, knees, legs, thighs, core, upper body, arms, hands, and head should be doing on every count. It is grueling, but so exhilarating when I am finally able to execute the step and do it well! At that moment the whole world is about learning how to perform a graceful but dynamic crossover break in the bolero, or a syncopated underarm turn with a ronde.

———

It is grueling, but so exhilarating when I am finally able to execute the step and do it well! At that moment the whole world is about learning how to perform a graceful but dynamic crossover break in the bolero, or a syncopated underarm turn with a ronde.

———

Like me, many other amateur dancers come to the studio straight from their offices, happy to put the workday behind them and eager to lose themselves in an activity completely separate from their jobs. Emmanuel's other students run the gamut from middle school teacher Jackie Soccodato to executives like Bonnie Wong, who works in private banking at JPMorgan Chase, and Nickie Maclusi, who works in business development at Shearman & Sterling, a major New York law firm. At one point, Jackie, Bonnie, Nickie, and I formed a little posse when we traveled to competitions to compete with Emmanuel. We cheer one another on during the Pro-Am events, and at the Open Professional Rhythm Championships held in the evenings we'll all yell Emmanuel's number. Emmanuel and Liana often win these championships or place second or third. Our posse serves as their traveling rooting section and revs up the crowd with our vocal support for our champions. I'm notorious for continually shouting Emmanuel's number at the top of my lungs.

After we're done competing for the day, the four of us rhythm and Latin gals will get dressed up and have drinks and dine together in one of the elegant hotel dining rooms. If we're at a resort, we'll hang out on the beach together, sunbathe, and talk through the highs and lows of our performances, completely relaxed after the stress of competition.

♪

In September 2010 a new ballroom event, the Sunshine State Dance Sport Competition, was held for the first time, organized by a top teacher and ballroom entrepreneur, Andrew Phillips. There are about twenty major and secondary competitions in the ballroom world, and if you're on the competition circuit, you want to compete in many of these so that you become familiar to the top judges, who will often take a few extra seconds to judge your performance. I knew the Sunshine State Competition would attract the top judges because of its venue: the newly renovated Fontainebleau Hotel in Miami Beach, Florida. I decided I had to go.

The Fontainebleau lobby was breath-taking, with shimmering bow tie marble floors, fluted columns, massive art deco chandeliers, and the famous "stairway to nowhere" rising alongside a glittering gold-tiled wall.

I'd always wanted to stay at the legendary Fontainebleau, which had been built in the 1950s when Miami Beach was the American Riviera. It had featured La Ronde Supper Club, which had a stage and dance floor that could be raised and lowered hydraulically. I couldn't wait to see how this iconic hotel had been refurbished. It didn't take too much to persuade the posse to join me in Miami Beach, and I talked Emmanuel and Liana into taking us. They were happy to do it because with four students it would be a profitable outing for them. (And it was, because Emmanuel and Liana won the Open Professional American Rhythm Championship at that competition and the top prize money.)

With cold weather settling in back in New York, all six of us were delighted to touch down in Miami. The Fontainebleau lobby was breathtaking, with shimmering bow tie marble floors, fluted columns, massive art deco chandeliers, and the famous "stairway to nowhere" rising alongside a glittering gold-tiled wall. The beachfront setting and elegant shops did not disappoint, although the ballroom where the competition was to take place was a little on the small side. Given the decision I had made, that was probably a good thing.

One of the dances I would be competing in was the mambo, the only dance that still unnerved me. But it was time to confront it. After all, I had come face-to-face with every one of my deepest fears on the ballroom floor, from my fear of losing control to my fear of failure. I had learned from ballroom dancing that whether in dance or in life, it's important to not hold anything back. Holding back may be a protective instinct for human beings, but it doesn't serve you well on the dance floor. Once, when I was trying to learn the maypole step for my samba (it's just what it sounds like: turning quickly in place, as if weaving a maypole), I kept losing my balance on the reverse turn. Emmanuel told me, "Sometimes you have to lose your balance to find your balance." When he said that, I knew I had to just "go for it" in order to learn how to execute that step.

The mambo had always been my most difficult dance. It starts on the two beat, which is confusing and not very intuitive. Making matters worse, mambo music is often cacophonous, with so many instruments and sounds going on that it's sometimes hard for me to find and follow the beat. I always dreaded doing the mambo in competition because, depending on the music that was being played, I was never sure I'd be able to hear the beat. Even if I did hear it, there was a good chance that I'd dance on the *wrong* beat.

———

I had come face-to-face with every one
of my deepest fears on the ballroom
floor, from my fear of losing control
to my fear of failure. I had learned
from ballroom dancing that whether
in dance or in life, it's important to
not hold anything back.

———

To add to my anxiety, my partner was Emmanuel, the
World Mambo Champion, and all eyes were usually on him
during a mambo heat. That meant all eyes were on me, too. If
I was dancing on the wrong beat, Emmanuel would have to
work extra hard to get me back on track. Sometimes I was so
far off that he would actually have to stop dancing and start
me up again. To my utter mortification, that had happened
more than once. After one of these debacles a ballroom judge
had joked to Emmanuel that he deserved a special award for
keeping me on the right beat. Painful as that was to hear, I
agreed with him.

In a last-ditch effort to avoid stressing myself out about
dancing the mambo, I had come up with a plan for the Sunshine State Competition: we should forget about a routine

altogether. No choreography—I would just follow Emmanuel's lead.

"Not having a routine will eliminate at least one thing that gets in the way of my hearing the beat and following you," I said. Emmanuel thought about it for only a few seconds before replying, "Sure! Let's try it and see what happens."

"Good," I said, although it felt like I started to sweat the instant he agreed. Still, I knew it was my only hope of taming the mambo. Without the distraction of a dance routine, I would have no choice but to be fully present and attuned to Emmanuel's signals. In the small Fontainebleau ballroom, there would be relatively few witnesses to the potential disaster of our improvised mambo. Jackie, Bonnie, and Nickie all thought the idea was bold and a little crazy— "Go for it!" they urged. Of course, *they* had carefully choreographed routines for all their dances.

On the day of the competition, I strolled around the ballroom and marketplace bazaar talking to the vendors, most of whom I now knew by name. I chatted with and received good wishes from top judges I knew from other competitions—Wendy Johnson, Eddie Simons, Michael Chapman, and Sam Sodano. Kristina Staykova, who had designed my peacock-themed rhythm dress, was also there with her own booth in the marketplace. She had recently refurbished that costume with even more peacock feathers and rhinestones. Before the competition, Kristina styled my hair (she called the look "reckless abandon") and did my makeup, which was artistic and extreme in its vibrant, glittery color. I was ready to dance.

As Emmanuel escorted me onto the ballroom floor for my first mambo, my heart started a sickening, nervous pounding. Those judges standing at the edge of the floor—I knew all of them—had seen me dance the mambo many times before. I could imagine some of them secretly wondering whether I'd be able to keep up with Emmanuel and dance on the right beat. Panicking a bit, I started to wonder, *How could I have dumped my routine?* The routine was my security blanket, a series of steps I practiced hundreds of times. For the mambo, I should have clung to every possible thread of that blanket.

When the music started, I took a deep breath, looked Emmanuel in the eyes, and prayed, "Please, God, let me hear the beat of the music so I can dance it!"

When the music started, I took a deep breath, looked Emmanuel in the eyes, and prayed, "Please, God, let me hear the beat of the music so I can dance it!"

Emmanuel signaled with a hard twist of his right hip that he was starting the action that would send his left foot forward, and I mirrored him by twisting my left hip to start the action that would send my right foot back on the two beat. I focused on counting in my head and stepping on the two-three-four beats, all the while following Emmanuel as he led me into basic mambo steps, swivels, free spins, hip twists, cross-body leads with an underarm turn, and wrap-arounds. At the end of the dance, he sent me into a dead drop straight down into his arms—what an adrenaline rush!

I thought dancing the mambo without a routine would be scary, but to my astonishment it was actually less scary than usual. Since I didn't have a routine, I couldn't antici-pate my steps or worry about being late. I had no time to think. I was dancing fully in the present. It was totally exhil-arating and, ironically, dancing fully in the present was the least scary place I had ever been when dancing the mambo in competition. The present was where I needed to be to dance mambo or any other dance. It was the only safe place to be—in dancing and in life.

I danced the mambo six times at the Sunshine State Dance Sport Competition, and won first place in all six heats! I had never done that before. To reward myself, I wandered through the marketplace bazaar afterward and purchased a beautiful sea-green rhythm dress studded with gold stones and long fringe. It was body hugging, sleeveless, backless, and more revealing than anything I had ever dared to wear.

After eight years of experiencing pure, unadulterated joy from my ballroom dancing, I was happier than I had ever been. I always thought that such joy would be the result of falling in love again after my husband died. My surprise was that I did fall in love, but not with someone else. I fell in love with myself, the person I had successfully avoided for so many years while I feverishly tended to the needs of others. The image of Ginger Rogers and ballroom dancing forced me to reengage with myself on all levels—mind, body, and spirit. It forced me to embrace, celebrate, and love myself, including the ten pounds I still want to lose. And in loving myself, I became a more loving person.

It doesn't matter what brings us joy. What matters is that we pursue our joy wholeheartedly, relentlessly, and with a sense of urgency. Like the people who perished on 9/11, we may not have the luxury of tomorrow. Or as Emmanuel put it, "I don't need to write down goals. I am the goal." In dance, and in life.

—

It doesn't matter what brings us joy. What matters is that we pursue our joy wholeheartedly, relentlessly, and with a sense of urgency.

—

CODA

Cha Cha

WHEN YOU DANCE—really dance—your feet are not just stepping through patterns. They connect you to the earth, and from the earth your dancing feet draw living vitality and power that radiates upward, flowing like an electric current between you and your partner at your joined hands, your gently touching arms, and your attentive gaze. That's connection.

The flirty cha cha is the perfect conduit for it. Practically announcing with a wink, "Here I come, baby," the cha cha moves you in and out of your partner's space. When he breaks back, she breaks forward into the space he was in. When she breaks back, he breaks forward into the space she was in. The lively but moderate tempo of the cha cha makes it feel playful to trade spaces this way, whereas the slower rumba feels sultry and the faster mambo feels intense. In the basic cha cha pattern, other than breaks, the partners move simultaneously in a triple step. It's this section that can help you develop real feeling for the contact of your feet with the earth. There's a simplicity to cha cha movement that allows you to focus on essentials. You don't have to project your body through long strides as you would in a smooth dance like the waltz. You don't have to worry about generating as much Cuban motion in the hips as you would in the rumba, or the kind of bounce you need in the samba. And you don't have to move your feet as quickly as you would in the mambo. You can relax into the game of moving together and using the floor as your ally.

The distinctive triple step of the cha cha came about because slower versions of Cuban mambo music left dancers with extra time between forward and back breaks. Simply holding in place would have been too static. They filled the extra time with a triple step called a chasse, a quick, staccato combination in which you step with one foot and your other foot seems to chase it on to its next step. People called this dance "triple mambo" for a time. Legend has it that the distinctive sound of women's shoes sliding across the floor, using it to generate the chasse, gave the new dance its name: two-three, cha-cha-cha, two-three, cha-cha-cha.

The cha cha was easier than the mambo for eager dancers to master, yet frisky enough to make a gal feel like a hot number and a guy feel like a cool cat. American pop culture of the 1950s and early '60s embraced the cha cha as fervently as a first love. But rock and roll broke up America's affair with the cha cha by offering something wilder and more rebellious. A different kind of earthiness took over social dancing, as partners let go of each other almost completely, kicked off their shoes, and tried to connect to each other as individuals moving to their unique beats, above and beyond patterns, outside conventional partnerships.

For many years, ballroom and Latin dances became the province of aficionados, competitors, and professional dancers. Generations grew up without experiencing the profound pleasure of taking the hand of an acquaintance or loved one and moving together to the music. Many would say, "I wish I had learned it. I wish I could." They would watch in wonder as glamorous professional dancers on television took nondancing stars of all ages in hand and taught them to control their feet and thus their bodies. Mastering the routines set many of the novice dancers free. Free of insecurities, free of excess weight, free of the constrictions of their jobs and images.

Dances like the cha cha or the samba or the elegant waltz can relight a vital spark in anyone. You'll feel connected to the music, to the earth beneath your feet, and to your partner. Most important, you'll connect with the deepest part of yourself. When that happens, you may never want to stop dancing. Why should you? Let joy be unconfined!

photo by Melody Reed, photographer

About the Author

Patrice Tanaka is cochair, chief creative officer, and *whatcanbe*™ ambassador for CRT/tanaka, an award-winning PR agency she helped co-found in September 2005. Her agency has been recognized as the "Best Agency to Work for in America" and "#1 Most Creative PR Agency in America." In her free time, Tanaka serves on the boards of several nonprofit organizations dedicated to helping women and girls and is a competitive ballroom dancer. She has received honors from industry and civic organizations including the Public Relations Society of America, Association for Women in Communications, New York Women in Communications and Girl Scout Council of Greater New York. A distinguished alumna from the University of Hawaii, Tanaka lives in New York City.